WHEN A

Loved One

Dies

BY SUICIDE

"When our family lost our son Zachary to suicide, we rediscovered the power of community, especially our Catholic community. The community embrace during those early months allowed us to find meaning in tragedy and helped us to move forward. This book is a welcome contribution to the faith journey that accompanies survivors of suicide loss and is a bright path forward for those turning to their faith during this terrible ordeal."

Dan Misleh
Executive Director
Catholic Climate Covenant

"During the last twenty years I've accompanied many individuals who have lost a loved one to suicide. As a lay minister and as a psychotherapist, how I wish I'd had this book to put in their hands! This is a long overdue, compassionate, and practical resource for people of faith trying to make sense of losing a loved one to suicide. These pages are filled with deep wisdom, accurate Church teaching, and realistic suggestions based on the latest psychological research to help survivors cope and heal in the aftermath of suicide."

Roy Petitfils
Licensed Professional Counselor
Author of *Helping Teens with Stress, Anxiety, and Depression*

"I could not put this book down! The Holy Spirit is truly alive in it under the mantle of the Catholic Church and in the raw honesty coming forth from the testimonies of people who have had a loved one die by suicide. Having lost our son, Thomas, to suicide in 2014, *When a Loved One Dies by Suicide* spoke to my heart in a new way that transcends the tragedy of suicide. This book will help you, too, move from grief to grace."

Anne Redlinger
Catholic Writer
San Diego, California

"It's an honor to endorse this book. Finally, we have an excellent pastoral and theological resource for survivors and pastoral care-givers who minister to them. Every hospital and behavioral health department should have this book to assist with the healing process of those who are grieving because of suicide loss."

Mike Garrido
Vice President, Mission Integration
Mercy Hospital
Miami, Florida

"My wife, Helene, and I lost our beloved son Ryan to suicide in 2011. This wonderful little book has greatly moved me, nine years later. *When a Loved One Dies by Suicide* conveys a message of spiritual clarity, reassurance, and hope through the eyes of parents and family members who have suffered the tragic loss of suicide. This book spoke to me, comforted me, and reassured me that as Helene and I continue to entrust ourselves to the loving hands of God, we are in those hands with Ryan."

John J. O'Malley
Professor of Psychology Emeritus
University of Scranton

"I have lost two children to suicide, one in 2006 and another in 2011. For anyone grieving such heart-rending loss, this book will be a steady help and great source of comfort. Each of the shared stories in this book illustrates that—with faith and loving support—a transformation from a life of intense grief to one of hope and healing, of posttraumatic growth, is truly possible."

Ann Marie McCrone
Grief Support Facilitator
St. Peter's Cathedral
Scranton, Pennsylvania

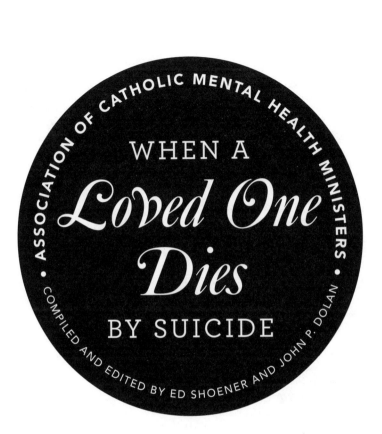

ASSOCIATION OF CATHOLIC MENTAL HEALTH MINISTERS

WHEN A

Loved One

Dies

BY SUICIDE

COMPILED AND EDITED BY ED SHOENER AND JOHN P. DOLAN

Comfort, Hope, and Healing
for Grieving Catholics

AVE MARIA PRESS AVE Notre Dame, Indiana

Scripture texts in this work are taken from the *New American Bible, revised edition* © 2010, 1991, 1986, 1970 Confraternity of Christian Doctrine, Washington, DC, and are used by permission of the copyright owner. All Rights Reserved. No part of the *New American Bible* may be reproduced in any form without permission in writing from the copyright owner.

Nihil obstat: Rev. Royce V.Gregerson, S.T.L.
          Censor deputatus

Imprimatur: Most Reverend Kevin C. Rhoades
          Bishop of Fort Wayne–South Bend
          August 28, 2020

Founded in 1865, Ave Maria Press is a ministry of the United States Province of Holy Cross.

www.avemariapress.com

Paperback: ISBN-13 978-1-64680-013-1

E-book: ISBN-13 978-1-64680-014-8

Cover image © iStock / Getty Images Plus.

Cover and text design by Samantha Watson.

Printed and bound in the United States of America.

Library of Congress Cataloging-in-Publication Data
Names: Shoener, Ed, editor. | Dolan, John (Bishop) editor.
Title: Responding to suicide : a pastoral handbook for Catholic leaders /
   compiled and edited by Ed Shoener and John Dolan.
Description: Notre Dame, Indiana : Ave Maria Press, 2020. | "Association of
   Catholic Mental Health Ministers." | Summary: "In this compilation,
   Shoener and Dolan share personal stories of their pain, insight, and
   comfort, along with important information from mental health experts and
   church leaders to help readers find the spiritual and emotional support
   they need after a loved one dies by suicide"-- Provided by publisher.
Identifiers: LCCN 2020030455 (print) | LCCN 2020030456 (ebook) | ISBN
   9781646800131 (paperback) | ISBN 9781646800148 (ebook)
Subjects: LCSH: Church work with the bereaved. | Suicide--Religious
   aspects--Catholic Church. | Pastoral theology--Catholic Church.
Classification: LCC BV4330 .R47 2020 (print) | LCC BV4330 (ebook) | DDC
   259/.428--dc23
LC record available at https://lccn.loc.gov/2020030455
LC ebook record available at https://lccn.loc.gov/2020030456

Contents

Introduction

SUICIDE AND OUR CATHOLIC FAITH

Deacon Ed Shoener
Diocese of Scranton

Suicide is a hard word. Suicide is a word you never wanted to have to think about. But suicide has now become a permanent part of your life.

Your love for the person who died did not end with the suicide of course. But your deep grief began then and there. And now, you want to somehow understand the suicide and find some way toward healing and a sense of normalcy.

You may cry and weep as you read this book. That's okay—tears help heal us. Tears wash away the pain, bit by bit. Tears remind us of just how much we love our family member or friend who has died by suicide.

The Church is weeping with you because what is true throughout our world is also true in the Church—many people understand your pain since they too have lost loved ones to suicide. In the Church, this group who understand includes bishops, priests, deacons, religious sisters and brothers, parents, siblings, grandparents, and spouses. Some of them have shared their stories in this book to try to help you through this time and lead you toward your particular path of healing.

Christ, who wept at the death of his friend Lazarus, also weeps with you. Yes, God is with you as you weep. He will always be with you. He will wipe away every tear from your eyes as Revelations 21:4 tells us, and "there shall be no more death or mourning, wailing or pain, for the old order has passed away."

Since my daughter, Katie, died by suicide in 2016, I have been with many Catholics who are grieving the death of a loved one by suicide. I have seen how their faith helped them. I have experienced the loving presence of Christ in my life as I learn to live with the suicide of my sweet daughter.

This small book will help you think about your loved one's suicide in the light of our Catholic faith. The stories and short essays reflect on how our Catholic faith helps us in three interrelated ways after the suicide of a loved one: (1) by healing us spiritually, (2) by comforting us in our ongoing grief, and (3) by giving us hope so we can serve others. These are not separate sequential steps; rather, our healing and our grieving are intertwined in hope as our lives are forever changed and transformed by Christ.

OUR FAITH HEALS US SPIRITUALLY

Jesus Christ can heal you and help you grow after the suicide of your loved one. You can lean on your Catholic faith to slowly heal. Suicide inflicts a deep spiritual wound. This spiritual wound causes you to suffer in ways you never imagined. It is a spiritual wound that can make you angry with God. You feel abandoned by God and his Church. It creates a deep spiritual loneliness that tears at your faith, your hope, and even your ability to love and accept love. This spiritual wound will take time to heal, but you will heal if you allow Christ to guide you on your journey to healing. And although it may be hard, if not impossible, to see right now, eventually out of this devastation you will even grow spiritually.

About a year after Katie died, my wife, Ruth, and I, along with our sons Ed and Rob and Rob's then-fiancée, Kate (now wife), went on a pilgrimage that Catholics from all over the world have been taking for a thousand years. We went on the Camino de Santiago, "the Way of Saint James," in northern Spain. Oftentimes it is simply called "the Camino" or "the Way." Pilgrims walk the Camino over many days, or even weeks, ending in the city of Santiago de Compostela, where there is an ancient cathedral that contains the relics of St. James the Apostle. The trip was a beautiful pilgrimage that brought our family closer together and a wonderful metaphor for the healing journey that we are all on after a loved one's suicide. We took one route, but there are many different routes that can be followed to get to Santiago de Compostela. A great tradition on the Camino is to greet and encourage fellow pilgrims as you walk by saying, "*Buen camino*," which means "good way." We found the greeting regularly returned.

We walked as a family. Some of us being faster than others, at times we walked with one person and then another, and sometimes each of us walked alone. Some of us spent a great deal of time in chapels along the way praying, and some spent less time. We also met other pilgrims along the way who were from all over the world, and on occasion we talked about our suffering, and I told everyone I met about my wonderful Katie. We were all together on the same path to the great cathedral in Santiago de Compostela.

When we reached the cathedral, we attended Mass and experienced Christ in the Eucharist and in the great community of faithful pilgrims that fill the cathedral every day. One of the most remarkable things about the cathedral is its magnificent thurible—the metal

xii   *When a Loved One Dies by Suicide*

container in which incense is burned during Mass. Made of silver and five feet in length, the thurible of the Cathedral of Santiago de Compostela is held by ropes suspended from the ceiling. During Mass servers pull on the ropes and swing the thurible from one side of the cathedral to the other so that the smoke and smell of the incense fills the entire cathedral, rising heavenward, even as do the prayers of all those gathered in that holy place. This was a dramatic and powerful element of our time at the cathedral.

Once we reached Santiago de Compostela, our long walk was over, and we were able to rest and heal our tired bodies. On this long pilgrimage each one of us found spiritual healing, in our own distinct way. And from there we went back to our everyday lives.

You can probably already understand why I told this story of the Camino de Santiago. After a suicide we begin a long and tiring journey. Many others have been on this journey before us, and sadly, many more will be on this journey after us. It is best to go with others, such as family, and on occasion to be open to strangers while we are on the journey. Don't be ashamed that you are on this journey. Do not be ashamed of your loved one who died by suicide. Talk about your grief, and talk about your loved one who died as you are on the way of healing. Take time to pray. Trust that time for rest will come again for you.

To heal you must set your intention to heal. You must begin the journey of healing and find your own way. You must put one foot in front of the other, even on days when you may not want to get out of bed. Your healing journey is not some random walk. Like the Camino, it is an intentional pilgrimage to find Christ in your suffering and to let Christ heal you.

And one day you will arrive at your destination and find healing. You will realize that all your prayers and tears and suffering rose up to God like burning incense. You will realize that your faith led you on this journey. You will rest in the love of Christ's Church.

Like the resurrected Christ, you are scarred by your spiritual wounds, but you will be healed. After the Resurrection Christ showed his scarred hands and side to Thomas and the other apostles. His wounds were healed, but the scars remained a part of him. The fact that he was scarred but healed helped others to believe. Likewise, your spiritual wounds will be healed, and as hard as this may be to see now, your spiritual healing will one day be a source of spiritual strength to others.

OUR FAITH COMFORTS US IN OUR GRIEF

Your grief is something that will be with you forever. Your longing for your loved one who died by suicide and your sadness caused by the realization that your loved one was in such deep pain that it led to their suicide never goes away completely. It will diminish in intensity and come and go, but it will never completely disappear. The grief has become a part of you. You will have to accept the suicide of your loved one, but that does not mean you will "get over" their death. You will find a way to integrate your grief into your life, and amazingly you will, one day, experience joy again.

Recall often your loved one's funeral, because a Catholic funeral always focuses on the death and resurrection of Christ. At your loved one's funeral, the whole Church prayed for them. Your loved one did not die alone—Mary and all the saints understood the pain they were in and accompanied them into the loving presence of Christ. A funeral is not the end but the beginning of our new relationship with our loved one who is now closer to Christ than any of us who are among the living.

The Church understands your grief and your concern for your loved one. The *Catechism of the Catholic Church* (*CCC*) teaches, "We should not despair of the eternal salvation of persons who have taken their own lives. By ways known to him alone, God can provide the opportunity for salutary repentance. The Church prays for persons who have taken their own lives" (*CCC*, 2283).

You can find comfort in the rituals of the Church. They can help you pray when you cannot pray on your own. Go to Mass even if you are not able to focus on the prayers or the readings or the preaching, because the holy angels that are present at every Mass will be with you and bring comfort to your soul.

Sometimes your only prayer will simply be "Jesus." If that is all you can pray, then just pray "Jesus." If you can pray a repetitive prayer, such as the Rosary, pray it. There is great power and comfort in repeating the prayers of the Rosary.

Consider simply sitting in the presence of Christ in quite adoration before the Blessed Sacrament. Stop by a church, sit quietly, and pour your grief out to Christ in the Blessed Sacrament. Christ knows what it is to suffer. In a special way his mother Mary is close to you because she too experienced the grief brought on by the painful and violent death of a person she loved deeply. Pray to Mary as you adore her son, and contemplate his suffering on the Cross. Mary will bring you great consolation as you grieve.

Do not give into the temptation to abandon your faith. That is the desire of the evil one—to draw you away from your faith. Cling to whatever piece of your faith, whatever small ritual or prayer, works for you. These are all gifts from the Holy Spirit to comfort you. Accept these gifts. These gifts from God will get you through this storm of grief and bring you to restful waters one day.

Death by suicide is not the end, and it does not break the bonds of love we had in life. All the ties of love and affection that knit us as one throughout our lives do not unravel with death. Christ was present through it all, in life and in death.

Death is transformed by Christ's death. Jesus has transformed the curse of death into a blessing. What the apostle Paul said so many years ago is still so true today: "We will all be changed, in an instant, in the blink of an eye, at the last trumpet" (1 Cor 15:51–52). Through Christ, death is transformed, and like Paul, we can say, "Where, O death, is your victory? Where, O death, is your sting?" (1 Cor 15:55). Our answer is that death is swallowed up in Christ's victory over death through his resurrection.

Our faith tells us that our loved one will be freed from all the pain that caused their suicide, freed from all their fears, freed from whatever attachment they may have had to sin—they will be purified of all of that. They will be purified of anything that made them less than the wonderful, beautiful, vibrant, and holy person that God created them to be.

What is said in the ancient book of Lamentations is our lament: "My life is deprived of peace, I have forgotten what happiness is; My enduring hope, I said, has perished before the LORD. . . . Remembering it over and over, my soul is downcast" (Lam 3:17–20).

Yet this scripture then says, "But this I will call to mind; therefore I will hope: the LORD's acts of mercy are not exhausted, his compassion is not spent; They are renewed each morning—great is your faithfulness! The LORD is my portion, I tell myself, therefore I will hope in him. The LORD is good to those who trust in him, to the one that seeks him; It is good to hope in silence for the LORD's deliverance" (Lam 3:21–26).

Because of these promises of God from ancient times, because of the power and love of Christ's death and resurrection, and because of healing presence of the Holy Spirit in our lives each day, we can clearly see that our loved one was a beautiful gift from God, that they will know the mercy and the love of God. Let your faith and hope in the resurrection of your loved one comfort you as you long for them and grieve.

OUR FAITH GIVES US HOPE

Christ will transform your suffering into hope. As we are spiritually healed by Christ and as we learn to live with our grief, we are also transformed with hope.

Out of your suffering and grief will come empathy, understanding, and a love for others who are suffering. Your suffering will be the source of strength to serve others.

You will be able to bring hope and consolation to those closest to you, to your family, when they suffer. You will bring hope and healing to people in your parish and your community, and to friends and neighbors. You will bring hope and strength to the Church because your suffering is joined to Christ's suffering and your compassion flows from his.

You will be able to bring the light of Christ into the darkness of suffering, into places you never thought you would be able to go. You will bring Christ's light not with a superficial sentimental kind of happiness but with the deep joy that comes from having experienced the healing love of Christ. Filled with hope and joy you will become less selfish and will want to share Christ's love with others.

Yes, this can happen for you. Right now, you may not believe it or see how this could happen, but that is the future that awaits you. Christ can and will transform everything to the good—even the darkness and evil of suicide.

In this book you will read stories from people about how they turned their suffering into service to others. They serve people with mental illness, they serve people who have lost loved ones to suicide, they serve their Church in a deeper and more meaningful way, and perhaps most importantly, they serve the suffering Christ by being better able to serve those who suffer in their midst every day.

Hope is the great theological virtue that allows us to place "our trust in Christ's promises and relying not on our own strength, but on the help of the grace of the Holy Spirit" (*CCC,* 1817). In time, we are filled with hope because we know we did not recover from our loved one's suicide on our own; we were only able to get through the pain and sorrow and find healing because of the grace of God moving in our lives.

We cannot remove all suffering and pain. We cannot cure mental illness. We cannot heal all traumas. We cannot prevent all suicides. Yet, we will be called to accompany people and to bring the love of Christ to them in the midst of these sorrows. Because we have gone through the dark valley with Christ by our side we can, with great confidence, assure others that Christ will be with them, as will his Church.

You will be able to offer the hope of Christ to others.

You will be the light of Christ in the world.

USE THIS BOOK TO PRAY A NOVENA

A novena is a series of nine days of prayer (or other units of time) asking for graces from God. There are eight chapters and a concluding reflection that follow this introduction. Read one each day for nine days, or perhaps one per week for nine weeks. When we are grieving, we can only take things in small doses, so think about what will be a good pace for you, giving you time to reflect and integrate what you read into your particular journey toward healing.

At the end of each chapter are four brief prayers for you, each directed to one person of the Blessed Trinity and the final one to the Blessed Mother. You may want to pray them all, only one, or some other number. Keep in mind that you are not alone in this. The Church prays with you, and our good and gracious God is with you always. Remember that "*the LORD is close to the brokenhearted, saves those whose spirit is crushed*" (Ps 34:19). Pray. Pray often. The Church and we who have written this book are praying for you.

> God the Father, who created your loved one who died by suicide, understands all things, even suicide, and holds you in his tender mercy.
>
> Our Lord Jesus Christ, who during his earthly life experienced suffering and profound pain, understands all that you and your loved one have experienced. Christ remains with you always.
>
> The Holy Spirit, works in and through the Church to guide and console you.
>
> Mother Mary, understands family life, experienced the death of her Son, and will lead you to his everlasting love.

1.

A Message for Sibling Survivors of Suicide Loss

LEARN TO SHARE YOUR STORY

Bishop John Dolan
Diocese of San Diego

This is a message about losing a sibling through suicide. Although my experience is unique to me, and my surviving siblings have their own stories, there is one common thread that we as Christians all share. Our identity as Christians is the key to finding joy even in the midst of pain after the loss of a loved one through suicide.

It was the first day of my eighth-grade year when we buried my brother Tom. I was thirteen years old. The parish church of St. Mary Magdalene was packed with family, friends, and many of my classmates from the School of the Madeleine. It was a day for prayer and grieving. My brother Tom Dolan died in Chino State Prison by his own hand. He hanged himself.

MY FAMILY AND MY BROTHER TOM

Tom and I grew up in a large family; he was number five of nine children, and I am number seven. We were a strong Catholic family living among equally large families in our neighborhood, and guided by our parents, we were all rooted in faith and community oriented.

Tom was a handsome, talented, cheerful young man. He seemed to be self-directed and showed evidence of success in his future. He excelled in sports, especially baseball, wrestling, bowling, and rock climbing. He was an artist. He loved art, playing guitar, and singing. Sadly, he also began to enjoy the party scene, which led him away from his first loves.

Soon after high school, Tom began to be more reclusive, hanging around with just a few of his drug friends. Even as a kid—I was in seventh grade when Tom was nineteen years old—I knew that he was hanging around with the wrong crowd. My parents were especially leery of one friend that Tom had invited to our house. It was clear that this friend, Scott, was going nowhere, and drugs seemed to be his only future path in life. For whatever reason, Tom seemed to lean in that direction as well. I had just returned from a Boy Scout trip when I learned that Tom and Scott were on the run from the law. My mom sat me down and explained what had occurred while I was away.

Apparently, Tom and Scott had been drinking and using drugs. Whether on impulse or by plan, they decided to rob the house of our next-door neighbor. That same evening, my parents learned of the incident and attempted to confront Tom and Scott. Unfortunately, Tom held a gun—which belonged to Scott—and urged my parents to step out of the way. Shocked, but grateful that Tom (not Scott) was the one in possession of the gun, my parents stepped aside. My brother and his friend made a run for it and, along the way, managed to rob a store. After a few days, Tom and Scott were picked up, and after a few months Tom landed in Chino State Prison. I do not know what happened to Scott.

We are not entirely sure why Tom had taken such a turn for the worse in his later high school years. It could have been simply hanging around the wrong crowd. It could have been something else. In reality, my oldest brother, Steve, was being treated for mental health–related issues and had been just coming off a long series of drug use himself. Perhaps Tom was also beginning to show signs of mental illness.

After Tom landed in prison, our family went to Chino, California, to pay him a visit. I was elated to see my brother for the first time since before my Boy Scouts trip. He looked cleaned up. He showed true contrition, and he seemed to be mending his ways. My parents were especially happy to know that Tom had been visited by a Catholic priest chaplain. After our visit, Tom and I became pen pals. I looked up to him and truly loved him. I really believed he was on his way to becoming the brother that I once knew and admired.

TOM'S DEATH AND OUR DEVASTATION

But then the horrible news came that Tom had hanged himself in his cell. What devastation! It did not seem possible! Just prior to his suicide, we were all blessed with the news that Tom's sentence was going to be reduced to just a few years. How could it be that this young man in his late teens could spiral so quickly? How was he able to show such signs of improvement and then allow this to occur?

A number of theories as to why Tom killed himself were floating in my mind. My first thought was that he was killed. But there was no evidence of foul play. Another thought was that he was abused in prison and he just couldn't take it. To this day, I still do not know why he hanged himself. All I know is that we were all devastated. I can still picture the pre-vigil, when my mother stared at Tom's body in the casket. My dad was staring at her as she gently touched Tom's body and began to weep. Then Dad began to cry. Soon all my siblings and I started up. That memory is deeply embedded in me.

I knew that my parents were devastated. I would often hear comments—and sometimes still do—that "my parents are strong, but they must be devastated to lose their child." Both are true. To lose a son is tragic. My parents never got over it. Even to this day, they rarely talk about Tom, unless they refer to happier days when our family was together camping, or singing around the piano, or gathered for evening supper.

BURYING OUR PAIN

My parents were born and raised in rural Iowa. They were unfamiliar with therapy and wary of psychology. They managed to move forward with trust in God and in each other. Outside of our common faith and family ties, counseling was not an option. And so my family buried our pain. We all tried to cope, but the pain would manifest itself in many ways. I witnessed among my siblings a loss of faith, hope, and love exhibited through excessive drinking, depression, and even another suicide. Trying to bottle their pain and sorrow, their lives showed signs of unrest. We were affected each in our own way.

As a thirteen-year-old boy, I was affected deeply by Tom's suicide, and my life took a sudden turn. My coming-of-age years, in which I should have discovered my identity and purpose, were stunted. Because of Tom's suicide, I put finding my identity and purpose on hold as I witnessed the devastation in my family, especially in the lives of my parents. Rather than just being me, I began to hold claim to a super-persona that looked like this:

Tom was a rock climber, so I took up rock climbing. Tom was a wrestler, so I took up wresting. Tom was in a bowling league, so I joined a bowling league. In each case, I tried to reach beyond his level. I tried to do everything that Tom did, but even better. Of course, I would not use drugs. My parents deserved better. In a nutshell, I needed to save my parents. I needed to be the defender and savior of my family. Even in my Confirmation year—the same year of my brother's suicide—I knew I needed to be a soldier for Christ. In fact, I selected St. Michael the Archangel—soldier and defender—for my Confirmation name.

During my high school years, as I lived this super-life, I recall my dad telling me more than a few times to just be myself. I brushed it off and continued on my journey to be more than Tom. Not me, John—just more than Tom.

After my junior year in high school, I blew out both of my shoulders in a summer wrestling league. This set me into depression. I was excelling in the sport and bonding wonderfully with my teammates. It meant everything to me. When I was told that I could no longer wrestle, I was lost. I thought, *Where do I go now?*

After sitting idle for a while, and without a sense of purpose, I too began to show signs of depression. In my senior year I was falling behind in my assignments and my grades began to slip. I never attempted suicide, but I hoped for death. The only thing that kept me going was the knowledge that my parents did not deserve to lose another son.

Rather than living in this world of depression, I started getting involved in our parish youth group. There I found a new set of friends, and I seemed to show some signs of leadership in the group. Even the parish priests took notice of me and began to inquire if I would consider becoming a priest. Of course, becoming a priest would fit well with my need to be a savior for my family. At that time, I never outwardly expressed a desire to be my brother Tom or to be a savior of the family. But subconsciously, the intent was there.

After graduation from high school I entered St. Francis Seminary on the University of San Diego campus to begin studies for the priesthood. The first time I saw a psychologist was when I entered the seminary. It was a necessary part of the application process, and after only one follow-up meeting to a procedural battery of psychological tests, I was seen as fit to enter the seminary. I recall my review including a concern about Tom's suicide and what effect it had on me. That was the only time I met a psychologist individually during my entire college career at St. Francis.

SURVIVING A SECOND SUICIDE

When I was nineteen years old, tragedy hit our family again. We had gathered for Thanksgiving dinner, the table was set, and we were waiting for my sister Therese and her husband, Joe, to arrive. Instead, the police showed up and told us the horrible news that Therese had hanged herself in a local canyon just hours earlier. Then the news got worse. The police officers told us that Joe was expected to tell my parents about my sister's death, but instead he died by suicide himself, having ended his life by asphyxiation in his car that same morning.

To this day, the particular reason for Therese's suicide is unclear to me. Apparently, there was marital hardship. That Joe killed himself hours after Therese died by suicide would seem to back that up. He left his own suicide note for my parents, but I never had the opportunity to read it.

My sister Therese was a few years older than Tom. She was a kind person who had a beautiful smile. She was introverted and talented. Like Tom, she played guitar and was an up-and-coming graphic artist. I used to enjoy spending time in her room drawing and painting alongside her. She would give me tips on drawing faces. I remember her saying, "Begin with the eyes. The eyes express everything!" She excelled in her talents, earning a master's degree from the University of California San Diego and becoming an art instructor at a Catholic school.

Our family knew that Therese's marriage seemed strained from the beginning. I remember thinking that she seemed to be in a rush to have a wedding, but it was her life and she seemed happy. The family never quite took to Joe, and I believe Therese knew that. Joe was in his forties, and Therese was still in her twenties. It was revealed later that Joe had been in prison, but Therese had only found out about his past after the wedding. I had heard from my parents that he was abusive toward my sister; I do not know how far the abuse went.

Though the specific motive for Therese's death is unclear, Therese was clearly distraught, and after Tom's suicide, she and others in our family had struggled with depression and suicidal thoughts.

TURNING AWAY HELP, COMPOUNDING MY PAIN

While this moment was obviously tragic for me, I managed to get through the Thanksgiving weekend and return to St. Francis the following Monday. Counseling was offered but not required. I turned down the offer and just pushed forward. Of course, I had managed to bottle up my pain. In fact, before the funeral of my sister and brother-in-law, I was already back in school. I hardly talked about her death with my friends at the seminary.

On the Monday following Thanksgiving, while walking to philosophy class, a fellow University of San Diego student reported to me how angry he was. He said his friend had been jogging in our canyon that weekend when he came upon a woman who had hanged herself. He said that his friend had suffered great trauma after seeing the sight and that he was "pissed" at the woman for making his friend suffer.

That was my sister he was talking about. Of course, I didn't have the courage to tell him. All I know is that I found myself staring at a statue of our Blessed Mother resting on top of the Immaculata church there on campus. I remember feeling a sense of peace as I let him express his feelings. It was as if Mary was saying, "Even in your pain, just be there for him." It was one of the most surreal yet profound moments in my life.

After a few months, I was in the running for the seminary's senior-class president. When I lost the election, I was told by a few seminarians that their decision not to elect me was based on my siblings' suicides. Needless to say, I was furious. I was mad at them; I was mad at the newly elected president; I was mad at Tom, Therese, and Joe; and I was mad at God. I stormed out of the seminary and to the end of a field at the University of San Diego where I could be by myself. There, I tore into God. I let loose! I asked God to just end my life then and there.

After a good cry, I went back to the seminary and went to bed. I wasn't sure what I was going to do the next day. I was still mad, embarrassed, and ashamed to be a victim of sibling suicide. I hated the fact that I was labeled as different. It hurt.

Somehow, the next morning, I managed to thank God for taking my anger. I justified my outburst by saying that God was big enough to take it, and he would probably rather have me yell at him than curse my friends. Once again, I pushed on.

Even after the suicides of Therese and Joe, I went without counseling. The rector of St. Francis Seminary suggested some therapy, but I passed on the offer. He never pursued it again.

I was later accepted to St. Patrick's Seminary in Menlo Park, California, for theological studies. Again I went through the necessary battery of tests for entrance, but the suicidal trend in my family did not come up as an issue. I continued on until my senior year, when one faculty member saw my psychological report and urged the faculty to confront me on my family's history. After their numerous requests for me to see their counselor, the faculty finally insisted on a psychological review. I was ready for ordination to the diaconate, and they wanted assurance that I would be ready to accept the challenges of ministry in the Church. Seeing no alternative, I begrudgingly went for counseling, and after six sessions I was given the green light to continue toward ordination. I was ordained to the diaconate and then to the priesthood on July 1, 1989, for the Diocese of San Diego.

FINDING HELP FOR MY WOUNDS

Only after having some normal up-and-down ministerial experiences as a young priest did I begin to see the value of seeking counseling on my own. As a thirteen-year-old boy, my maturation was stunted, and as a young priest it was finally dawning on me that I had to deal with this identity crisis.

I discovered in just a few sessions that the daily routine of priesthood was not fitting nicely with the savior image that I had hoped for. Admittedly, many young priests struggle with a savior complex, and most are able to quickly realize that there is only one true Savior of the world. Unfortunately for me, it took a little longer. I think this was due in large part to posttraumatic stress I experienced after my brother's suicide.

I requested a leave of absence from ministry from my bishop. Moved by the grace of God, I began to review my life. This meant going back to my beginnings.

Returning to my Baptism, where I was born again as a beloved child of Christ, I re-presented myself as his Father's son. For the first time as a priest, I took seriously my identity as a Christian in the fullest sense of the word. I was suddenly more at peace with myself than I had ever been. Reclaiming my share in the divinity of Christ, who humbled himself to share in my broken humanity, I was ready to hear the words of my dad: "Be yourself!" During the leave of absence, I decided to see a counselor on a regular basis. I also found a spiritual director and reconnected with some of my old priesthood friends. To this day, I maintain all three avenues of support. This support system allows me to stay focused on my identity as a Christian. To know who I am means to know where I am going.

After returning to ministry, I threw myself into the life of my parish community with a fervent love for the Lord and his Church. My intent was to remain in parish ministry for the rest of my priestly life. God had other plans. Although my journey as bishop today can be heavily administrative, and although I am not embedded in the joys of parish life, I am more joyful than ever. I abide in his love who has loved me first. Sharing in the divinity of the one who humbled himself to share in my humanity is joy enough for me. This is both my identity and my journey. In order to help me abide in my Christian identity and mission, I pray. I pray a lot. I stay connected with our Blessed Mother, I celebrate the sacraments, and I pursue the virtuous life with a special focus on faith, hope, and love.

FINDING PEACE IN CHRIST

I am back living in an apartment at St. Francis Seminary on the University of San Diego campus. Each day, I walk on the campus praying the Rosary. Halfway through, I stop at the field where I cried and cursed at God on that night in the seminary. The field is now replaced by the Joan B. Kroc Institute for Peace and Justice building. There, I now thank God for peace. I offer a thanksgiving of peace, not because I'm a bishop or even a priest. I thank God for gracing me with the profound gift of being his son. I am his beloved. So too are my brother Tom, my sister Therese, and her husband, Joe. As I have found peace, may they rest in peace.

This is my story. My parents and my siblings each have their own stories as they are each survivors of suicide loss. If you are a survivor of one who died by suicide, you will have your own story. Tell your story. It will only bring growth. But if your story does not begin and end with being yourself, with the unique Christian self that God has made you to be, your journey will be difficult and your story will be incomplete. Christ never wanted our journeys to be difficult. In him, even with tragedies and daily crosses, we can find joy. Only in Christ will we have complete joy.

Key Points

- Grief does not go away, no matter how much we try to hide it.
- Grief affects everyone differently.
- We each need to tell our own story.
- We need to accept help from many places: a professional counselor, a bereavement group, a spiritual director or support group, and caring, attentive family and friends.

Prayers for the Way

After praying one or more of these simple prayers, sit in silence and contemplate God's presence. Open your heart and mind to God's peace.

> Heavenly Father,
> as the psalmist said, *You know all my thoughts.*
> Should I reach out to a counselor or other mental health
> professional for support? Amen.

> Lord Jesus,
> you helped people understand God by telling stories;
> give me courage to share my story with those who can
> help me in this journey of grief
> and with those whom I can help by sharing it. Amen.

Holy Spirit,
Grant the leaders of our Church the wisdom, compassion, and courage to befriend and walk alongside those who are grieving the suicide of a loved one. Amen.

Mother Mary,
You know how important family is during times of stress; guide our family to support each other during this time of deep sorrow and pain. Amen

2.

A Grief Revealed and Redeemed

THE SUICIDE OF MY SISTER, MARY ANNE POPE

Msgr. Charles Pope
Diocese of Washington, D.C.

My sister, Mary Anne Pope, was born on April 2, 1960, the first child of Charles and Nancy Pope. Mary Anne was tragically afflicted with mental illness from her earliest days. Because she did not speak a word until she was well past two, and even then only at home, my parents knew something was wrong. Discretion and brevity limit what I intend to share here, but even as little children, my brother, George, and I knew something was very wrong with our sister. Her erratic behavior made her shift from moments of fearful shyness to rather exotic actions that were either violent or just strange. Indeed, Mary Anne was deeply troubled.

MENTAL ILLNESS AFFECTS THE WHOLE FAMILY

My sister, Mary Anne, had a pathological shyness that led her to shut down in the presence of others outside the home. The counselor at her elementary school spoke of Mary Anne as "disturbed" and insisted on psychiatric care for her by the time she was six. I remember when I was very young my mother bringing Mary Anne to her counselor. She explained that Mary Anne was "shy" and that her friend was helping her feel better.

At one point in early 1970, aware that Mary Anne felt isolated in the house with two brothers and desperately wanted a sister, my parents even went so far as to seek to adopt a baby girl. They filed paperwork and came very close, but the plan ultimately fell through and we never had a baby sister. By age eleven Mary Anne was running away from home. During this period and throughout her lifetime my parents made many sacrifices for Mary Anne, both financial and personal, to ensure her care.

When Mary Anne was thirteen, my parents found such deeply disturbing plans in her diary that mental health professionals advised and insisted that she had to be hospitalized. She spent the remainder of her life in fifteen different mental hospitals and six different group homes. Her diagnosis was paranoid schizophrenia.

She was often able to visit with us and even stay over on weekend passes. She had stretches during which she was stable, but soon the voices and dreams that afflicted her would return. Her psychotic episodes often led to running away, outbursts of violence, vandalism, shoplifting, setting fires, and cutting her wrists and other attempts at suicide.

Through all these years, my parents, in their grief and love, fought very hard for her, and they insisted she get the care she needed, despite insurance and governmental systems that increasingly consigned the mentally ill to life on the streets. This battle often led my parents to various courts and generated much correspondence with insurance companies, state mental health officials, and private hospitals where my sister was confined.

On one critical occasion my mother was summoned to a mental institution where my sister was residing. Mary Anne was standing on the roof of the five-story building, planning to jump. Police and fire officials were trying to call her off the edge. In the midst of this, my mother sensed the Lord speaking to her these words: "Mary Anne is more my daughter than yours. Whatever happens today, I want you to know that I love her and that she is in my care."

UNDERSTANDING AT THE LAST

Mary Anne died in a fire in the winter of 1991 at the age of thirty-one. At the time, I was thirty years old and an associate pastor at my first parish assignment. The fire investigators concluded that the fire was no accident and declared her death a suicide. Indeed, Mary Anne had set fires before when the voices told her to.

A great sadness in my life is that it took Mary Anne's death for me to recognize her dignity and see her true suffering. I had often avoided talking to her. She often tried to speak of her unusual dreams and her need for attention, but I made excuses and privately complained to my parents of her unwanted requests to talk.

But four days after her death I looked right into the face of her pain. The funeral directors explained that they had made her presentable enough for the immediate family to briefly view her body. They explained, however, that her features were delicate since the fire had singed her upper body. Thus they could not work much on her appearance or adjust the expression on her face. We gathered, for a last look, and it was then that I saw it. She had clearly died weeping. Yes, I could see the pain on her face as her body lay in the casket, and I wept deeply when I saw her. All of us did. Poor Mary Anne, poor, poor Mary Anne. It was a grief revealed. A very deep grief. Her life must have been riddled with grief, with suffering and grieving for a life she would never have.

How could I have missed my sister's grief for all those years? Was it my fear of her? Was it my annoyance? Perhaps it was my frustration at not being able to do anything to make my sister better. But such grief I had missed.

She had often talked of her dream to get well, marry, and be happy. I thought it was a crazy dream. But more likely it was her crying out, an expression of her grief and her pain at her tormented dreams and the voices that filled her mind with irrational fears. She just wanted to be well, normal, and happy. I missed all this; I missed her pain. But that day, looking one last time at her, I saw it, fixed there in her final expression. *Mary Anne*, I thought, *how little I really knew you or understood your pain. I am so sorry I missed it. I am sorry I did not understand. I am so sorry it took your death for me to know your grief and sorrow. May it never again be so, dear Mary Anne, that I miss the dignity of those close to me who suffer.*

Not long after her funeral, perhaps a day or two, I was celebrating a daily Mass and it was for her repose. Just after Communion, as I was purifying the vessels, I heard my sister's voice. It was not some internal conviction—it was a voice, her voice. She said, "I'm okay now, Charlie." To be clear, I am not one who hears voices or sees things. Yet so certain was I that I had heard a real voice, I asked the congregants, "Did you hear that?" I received only blank stares and a few looks that said no.

But I knew what I had heard. It was a consolation I did not think I deserved. She could never have said "I'm okay now" in this world. It rang true, and it sounded like her manner of speaking. Yes, I was sure it was her. Thank you, Lord, for that undeserved grace, which continues to bless my life!

THE RIPPLING EFFECTS OF DEATH BY SUICIDE

Suicide, of course, is a crushing blow for family members who experience such loss. This is so even in the cases of clear mental illness, as with my sister. My mother carried a special burden that I suppose only a mother knows. In the weeks and months that followed Mary Anne's death, she often wept and said simply, "My daughter, my beautiful daughter Mary Anne."

Sadly, my mother's grief grew steadily worse, causing her struggle with alcohol to worsen. She had been something of a drinker all her life, but it was mostly maintenance and self-medication. Through her forties and early fifties she had been a popular and successful schoolteacher at the local Catholic school. But her grief caused her to retire the year after my sister's death. At this point my mother's alcoholism went fully active and she became increasingly incapacitated: car accidents, medical issues, treatment centers, and attempt after attempt to get free—all the tragic stuff of alcoholism.

In all of this I strove not to forget the lesson my sister had taught me. While at times I was angry at my mother for her drinking, I did not want it to take her death for me to see and honor her grief, pain, and dignity. I went steadily to Al-Anon meetings to stay sane myself, and I honored my mother's many struggles to get free. I saw that her grief was something to be respected and not dismissed.

The life of my mother, Nancy Pope, ended tragically and suddenly on a cold February day in 2005. My father had looked away for only a brief moment, going into the kitchen to make a sandwich, and Mom wandered out into the cold and into the face of an impending snowstorm. Incapacitated by alcohol and disoriented, she died that night of hypothermia. We found her body only after three days of searching, when the snow melted a bit. She had died almost a mile away, near the edge of the woods. In her death it was a grief revealed: it was *her* grief—her deep, deep grief, a sorrow that stretched back some fifteen years to my sister's death.

My father never quite forgave himself for letting Mom slip away. The open front door was a first sign of trouble—a troubled night that grew increasingly awful as our frantic searching on a dark, frigid, and snowy night brought the steady and awful awareness that she was gone. Yes, those memories haunted my father.

In the months that followed, he often wondered how he could go on when half of him was gone. He often spoke of wanting to be with his Nancy, and he was gone within two years. His congestive heart failure worsened in those two years, and my dad, Charles Pope, died in 2007, literally and figuratively of a broken heart. It was a grief revealed.

After my father's death in 2007, and except for essential papers related to his estate, I simply boxed up most of his papers and stored them in the attic of my rectory for future attention. A few years later I was sorting through those boxes. Among his effects were many papers, both his and my mother's. In particular, I was struck by the poignant file that was simply labeled "Mary Anne." My father wrote this on the frontispiece of her file:

> Mary Anne Pope was our first child.
> She led a tortured existence during a short life
> and fought hard against great odds.
> We remember her for her courage.

As I read the historical data and my own parents' touching recollections of Mary Anne within the file, I could not help but be moved too by their own pain. Such a heavy grief punctuates each page. I give them great credit for the fact that they insulated the rest of us, their three sons, from the most dreadful details of Mary Anne's struggle. They kept their pain largely to themselves and stayed available to us. It is true that there were episodes we had to know about, but as a young boy and teenager I saw in my parents only strength and stability when it came to this matter.

Something of their pain is evident in those short lines of my father on the cover of her file. It was their grief revealed.

JESUS UNDERSTANDS SUICIDE: MARY ANNE CAN SEE THE GLORY OF GOD

An old spiritual says, "Nobody knows the trouble I've seen. Nobody knows but Jesus." And it is a mighty good thing that he *does* know. Sometimes the grief is too heavy even to share, even to put into words. But Jesus knows all about our troubles. As I have said, I deeply regret that I did not understand my sister's grief or pain until she died. My parents too often carried their pain quietly, and I cannot say I ever really knew their pain until I saw the file labeled simply "Mary Anne." But I am glad of this much: Jesus knew.

It is true, my sister, Mary Anne, died in a suicidal fire. But she was just too mentally ill and tormented by voices to be fully responsible for it. All that matters to me is that Jesus knew. She often called on him, and one fiery night when the pain was too great, I am convinced in faith that he called her home as if through fire (see 1 Corinthians 3:15).

Something tells me that I will have to get an appointment to see Mary Anne in heaven, since she will be close to the throne of God. Jesus says, "And the last will be first" (Mt 19:30). Mother Mary says that God lifts up the lowly (Lk 1:52). Yes, those who have suffered much but with faith will be exulted in heaven and be closest to God. My parents too surely saw their glory increased through their sufferings (see 2 Corinthians 4:10–15).

There is a beautiful line in the book of Revelation that refers to those who have died in the Lord: "He will wipe every tear from their eyes, and there shall be no more death or mourning, wailing or pain, [for] the old order has passed away. The one who sat on the throne said, 'Behold, I make all things new'" (Rv 21:4–5).

For my brave parents and courageous sister, who all died in the Lord but who died with grief, I pray that this text has already been fulfilled and that they now enjoy everything that is new, their tears are wiped away, and their grief has been redeemed.

Key Points

- It can take time to understand mental illness and suicide.
- Christ loves and understands people who had a mental illness and died by suicide.
- The death of a loved one by suicide is not something you "get over." It is a grief you will always live with.
- Give your grief to Christ.

Prayers for the Way

After praying one or more of these simple prayers, sit in silence and contemplate God's presence. Open your heart and mind to God's peace.

God our Father,
I know the pain that led my loved one to suicide
will pass away because you make all things new.
Wipe every tear from my eyes and from all who love
her [him]. Amen.

Lord Jesus,
Like those who live with a mental illness,
you were *a man of suffering, familiar with pain*
and *held in low esteem* (Is 53:3).
Help me to see the dignity of those close to me
who suffer. Amen.

Holy Spirit,
Help all members of our Church better understand
psychological disorder, mental illness, and suicide.
Fill our hearts with compassion and courage to act.
Amen.

Mother Mary,
You said, "God lifts up the lowly,"
when the angel came to you,
announcing the coming of Jesus.
I am suffering deeply and am as low as I have ever been;
carry me to your son who will lift me up. Amen.

3.

The Suicide Death of My Daughter, Katie

Deacon Ed Shoener
Diocese of Scranton

> We know that all things work for good for those who love God.
>
> —Romans 8:28

I am told everyone reacts differently when the knock comes at your door and you find out your child is dead. It was a knock that my wife, Ruth, and I hoped would never come—but one that for more than eleven years we had worried would come.

It was a few minutes before midnight on a warm Wednesday night in August. The doorbell suddenly started ringing rapidly, and there was loud knocking on our front door. I was upstairs in our bedroom with Ruth, and we were just getting to sleep. I said to Ruth, "This can't be good."

Ruth got to the door first and opened it. She said nothing, but she looked at me startled. I got to the door to see two police officers and immediately knew why they were there. Not a word was spoken until I asked, "It's Katie, isn't it?"

The officers came in, and we walked silently to the kitchen, in shock but strangely composed. We all sat at the kitchen table, and I answered their questions. I was given the phone number of the officer in Ohio who found Katie and who was conducting the investigation. Katie lived near Columbus; we lived then and still do in Scranton, Pennsylvania. I called the officer immediately.

The officer in Ohio told me Katie died from a gunshot to her head. He had to ask difficult questions for the investigation. I assured him it was suicide—not a murder. I explained that Katie had lived with bipolar disorder for more than eleven years. She had attempted suicide before and struggled with intense suicidal thoughts. I asked him when we could bring her body home. The detective explained that the county coroner needed to conclude the investigation before we could do that.

I begged him to please finish the investigation quickly—that we wanted to bring our little girl home. It was at this point that I began to feel pain through the shock. It came slowly at first. Some tears as I talked to the officer. Ruth and I looked at each other, and we were just so, so sad. But we kept ourselves under control, showed the officers out, and thanked them for being so kind. We said we knew it was not easy for them to give parents this news. Then they quietly left our house.

More pain than I had ever felt hit me then, and hit hard. Ruth put her head down on the table. She weakened under the pain. She just cried and cried and cried inconsolably.

I had never known what it is to wail. It goes beyond tears. It is visceral. It is primordial. It comes from a place most of us never know exists within us. It is tears and screaming and physical pain. I went out on our deck and pounded our wooden table. I screamed and sobbed. Our son Bill built the table and made it strong and sturdy. I don't know how long I pounded on it. I pounded until I was exhausted.

At some point Ruth and I fell into each other's arms. Two became one. We needed each other. We were one stream of tears, like blood flowing from a wound. There is nothing sentimental about love at this moment. It is raw. It is horrible. Yet, in the face of death, it is life giving. It is strong, and it goes beyond all understanding. No words are spoken. Words are not possible or needed. Love is needed.

KATIE'S MENTAL ILLNESS

Eventually Ruth and I started to talk. We did not know what else could have been done. Katie had done everything she was told to do by her doctors. She took all her medicines. She did not use drugs and was not addicted. Ruth talked to Katie every day—every single day. Katie's family loved her. She loved all of us, and she had many friends. She had recently graduated with her MBA from the Fisher College of Business at Ohio State University and wanted to work in human resource management because she loved helping people succeed.

We knew that Katie did not want to die by suicide. She wanted to live. She had attempted suicide before, and she was afraid of it. She had checked into a hospital several times when the suicidal thoughts were intense. She knew that suicide makes no sense. But mental illness is not rational. This illness told her that she was terrible, a burden, that no one liked or loved her, and that she was a useless mistake. She was in deep and irrational pain.

Mental illness is as evil and unrelenting as cancer, heart disease, or any other malady. For many people it can be treated and managed. Katie was treated by therapists and psychiatrists, and she took medicines for her type 1 bipolar disorder. Like chemotherapy for cancer, which can help people live longer than they would have without the chemotherapy, the medicines kept Katie alive for many years. But in her last year the medicines slowly stopped working. Her mental illness overwhelmed her and became lethal.

GOD'S GRACE AND KATIE'S OBITUARY

Ruth and I finally went to bed the night our daughter died, but sleep was impossible. Full-on dad instincts kicked in for me. I felt a need to do what I could for my little girl. I got up and called the funeral director in the middle of the night. We talked about getting her home, about making funeral arrangements, about all the things you never want to do for your child. But at this moment you do them—and you want to do them well. Katie still needed to be taken care of.

I decided I needed to write Katie's obituary. Ruth asked me what I was doing at the computer. It was the middle of the night and only a couple of hours since the police knocked on our door. How, she wondered, could I possibly be able to write anything? But I wanted our friends, neighbors, and parishioners to know what happened so there would not be any gossip or hushed talk. I wanted them to know that Katie was a good girl who had a terrible illness. So, with the grace of God, I wrote Katie's obituary that night.

> Kathleen "Katie" Marie Shoener, 29, fought bipolar disorder since 2005, but she finally lost the battle to suicide on Wednesday in Lewis Center, Ohio.
>
> So often, people who have a mental illness are known as their illness. People say that "she is bipolar"

or "he is schizophrenic." Over the coming days as you talk to people about this, please do not use that phrase. People who have cancer are not cancer, those with diabetes are not diabetes. Katie was not bipolar—she had an illness called bipolar disorder. Katie herself was a beautiful child of God. The way we talk about people and their illnesses affects the people themselves and how we treat the illness. In the case of mental illness, there is so much fear, ignorance, and hurtful attitudes that the people who suffer from mental illness needlessly suffer further.

Our society does not provide the resources that are needed to adequately understand and treat mental illness. In Katie's case, she had the best medical care available, she always took the cocktail of medicines that she was prescribed, and she did her best to be healthy and manage this illness. And yet, that was not enough. Someday a cure will be found, but until then, we need to support and be compassionate to those with mental illness, every bit as much as we support those who suffer from cancer, heart disease, diabetes, or any other illness.

Please know that Katie was a sweet, wonderful person who loved life, the people around her—and Jesus Christ.

Early that morning we made the calls you never want to make to your children. We called Katie's three brothers—Rob, Bill, and Eddie—to tell them their sister died by suicide. It was hard to hear the anguish, deep sorrow, and weeping from them.

I sent out an email to my colleagues at my business with the obituary and asked for their patience while I took time for Katie's funeral. I also sent an email with the obituary to the staff at St. Peter's Cathedral in Scranton, where I am a permanent deacon. And then

I went to the 8:00 a.m. Mass at the cathedral—the daily Mass I regularly attend.

CLINGING TO CHRIST, BROKEN FOR US

I was drawn to the Eucharist that morning with the strongest pull I had ever felt to attend a Mass. I entered the sacristy and saw Fr. Jeff Walsh and others talking about the news of Katie's death. They were surprised to see me. But where else would I go to find solace?

I asked to preach and explained to the small congregation why I needed to be at the Mass that morning. I read Katie's obituary— slowly, so that I would not sob and be incoherent—because it was important that they heard the message clearly.

Like the love between Ruth and me when we had received the news just a few hours earlier, there is nothing remote and sentimental about the love that Christ offers at Mass. His love, then as always, was direct, and I felt it. His passion and death were united to Katie's death and to my grief during that Mass. He held me up. He was with me. Christ went into my darkness, like walking into a tomb, to be with me. Katie was broken, I was broken, and Christ's body was also broken for us at the altar, as it is at every Mass. Christ was suffering with my family and me. His presence in the Eucharist was never more real to me.

At the end of Mass, I went down the aisle to greet the small group of people who attend the morning Mass. I needed to be surrounded by this small Christian community that I worship with each day. Again, it was not remote and sentimental; it was instead direct and real. All pretenses fell away.

In a community united in Christ, there is grief and sorrow, yet there is also strength and love; we lift one another up. Even if it was only a simple "I am so sorry," I could see in my community members' eyes the love of Christ as they said it. I knew once again Christ was broken for me by their compassion and loving presence.

I was scheduled to see my spiritual director, Fr. Jim Redington, for our monthly meeting that morning right after Mass. I kept the appointment. I walked the few blocks from the cathedral to the Jesuit residence at the University of Scranton, where my spiritual director lives. I told him about Katie. He knew how it felt to lose someone you love to suicide, telling me his brother died this way.

I am a spiritual director myself, and one of the fundamental beliefs about spiritual direction is that in every session there are three people: the directee, the director, and the Holy Spirit. Usually the directee does most of the talking, the director asks questions and offers guidance, and both listen in their hearts for the Holy Spirit. At our session that morning, we went into the small chapel of Fr. Jim's residence and simply sat in adoration of the Eucharist. I could not talk, and he knew there was nothing he could say that would help right then. Only the Holy Spirit spoke that morning. We were enveloped in love.

I was given the gift of God's peace on the most horrible morning of my life: at Mass, with the support of my faith community, and while in eucharistic adoration with a holy priest who understood my pain. The peace of the Lord was with my spirit.

THE VIRAL OBITUARY

The rest of that day was filled with calls and visits from family and friends, all deeply appreciated. That afternoon I went to meet with our funeral director to work out the details of the funeral. Ruth stayed at home to be with our family. I selected a white casket for Katie. White is the color of hope—hope in the Resurrection.

Among the many other things that had to be done, we also put the details of the funeral into Katie's obituary and sent it to the local newspaper for publication in both the hard copy of the newspaper and in the online version. It appeared the next day.

I had hoped the obituary would encourage an open and honest conversation about mental illness and Katie's suicide in our small town of Scranton, but what actually happened was totally unexpected. The response to Katie's obituary was incredible. It went viral in social media. It was picked up by newspapers throughout the United States and around the world. There was television and radio coverage. Katie's obituary was seen by millions of people, as headlines appeared in places near and far.

> She "Loved Life": A Grieving Father Wrote Openly about Suicide and Mental Illness in Daughter's Obituary
>
> —*Washington Post*[1]

> Katie Died by Suicide in a Bipolar Crisis and Her Father Wrote in the Obituary a Message to Humanity
>
> —*Visão*, Lisbon, Portugal[2]

> Parents Use Daughter's Obituary to Discuss the Stigmas
> around Mental Health
>
> *—Yahoo News*[3]

> Grieving Father's Commonsense Message about Mental
> Illness Is a Wake-Up Call
>
> *—Dallas Morning News*[4]

> From the United States Comes a Dramatic Story and
> a Very Strong Invitation to Rethink Our Way of Relat-
> ing to Those Suffering from Mental Disorders in "She
> Loved Life—a Father in Mourning Writes of the Suicide
> of Daughter with a Mental Illness,"
>
> *—Urban Post*, Livorno, Italy[5]

> On the Deacon's Daughter Who Died by Suicide: "God
> Will Use This Death to Help Others Come Out of the
> Shadows"
>
> *—The Deacon's Bench*[6]

> This Father Used His Daughter's Obituary to Make an
> Important Point about the Way We Treat People with
> Mental Health Issues
>
> *—The Independent*, United Kingdom[7]

I am convinced, beyond any shadow of doubt, that God used Katie's obituary to deliver his message of love. God did not create Katie to have a mental illness and die by suicide; he created her to be the beautiful and vibrant person that we all knew and loved. Yet we live in a broken world where there is sin, illness, and death. All this evil will be completely defeated in eternal life, but evil is also overcome every day in this life, as God pours out his love on us in the small things of life, such as Katie's obituary, as a sign of what is to come in eternal life. God overcame Katie's tragic death by using her obituary to help people understand that he is with them in their struggle with mental illness and he has mercy on those who die by suicide.

Some people took the time to write touching notes about what Katie's obituary meant to them on her obituary page at Legacy.com;[8] there were thousands of comments on Facebook pages, in various blogs, and in the comment sections of online newspapers. Here are just a few examples:

> I have lost many family and friends to suicide caused by a mental illness, and frankly, no one wants to talk about it. It's shameful, you're frowned upon, and you are labeled as being crazy. Well this is a very common illness that needs to be addressed, and this obituary will hopefully sway people to open up and talk about it before we lose more lives to this battle. I pray that as unfortunate as this is that even now God is using this for a good divine purpose, to educate others to be compassionate, to avoid being quick to judge because it can happen to you or anyone. May God shower you all with his comfort and strength knowing Kathleen's not suffering anymore and that the way she left this earth is not in vain; there is a divine purpose, and it started with Kathleen's obituary.
>
> —Anonymous

> As someone who has struggled with depression, I have often found it difficult to speak to people about my illness due to the stigma and ignorance that surrounds it. Thank you for what you have written, thank you for helping to dispel the negativity surrounding mental illness, thank you for helping us. May the Lord bless you and keep you.
>
> —Baton Rouge, Louisiana

We need more people discussing the realities of struggling with a mental illness and, just as you say, that it can be as difficult, painful, and sometimes terminal as any other serious illness. I am bipolar, and it's a constant battle. People have a difficult time understanding how I struggle, and the horrible pain of depressive episodes or cycling so much that my thinking is only realistic when I have some stability, on meds, and the challenge to even getting stable enough to mimic a decent life, at least for a while. We need to break through the stigma. Most people are afraid of the term. They usually conjure images of people being psychotic, running through the streets, naked. They don't realize the many, different facets of BP. I hope the discussion continues.

—San Jose, California

I am twenty-two years old and have bipolar disorder. I was diagnosed last year but have struggled since I was fourteen. I wish I had known Katie, because our stories are incredibly similar. I love God with all my heart, as Katie did. I struggle every day, and the stigma behind bipolar holds me back from getting all the support I need. Katie's life brought so much joy and learning to others, and her passing has brought healing and hope to many. I think that's the best kind of life well lived, even though her pain was greater than she could bear.

—Anonymous

Your touching story about Katie's life and her struggles with bipolar disease has led me to reach out for help for the first time (I am fifty-three). Katie's story has greatly impacted my life and the lives of many others that suffer from bipolar disease.

—Cheboygan, Michigan

I read Kathleen's story, and it brought me back to when I was a teen. I, too, suffered in silence my whole life. We had so much in common. I did the same thing in high school with the pills and slashing, being on meds for years. I've seen therapists, yet nothing has helped with my disorder. I've been suicidal many times, and I'm afraid that day will happen. I hope there's a cure before I give up the fight. I'm only forty-eight. So sorry for your loss. I know exactly how she felt.

—Halifax, Nova Scotia

My prayers to you and your family, may God comfort you. You have lived through my greatest fear. My twenty-one-year-old daughter has been fighting bipolar since she was twelve. We have seen her thru suicide attempts, crippling depression, self-harm, and hospitalizations, interspersed with periods of stability, joy, and shining talent. My daughter is stable for now, but there is always the fear. I have shared your post with my friends and family, as you have so eloquently expressed what this is like. Thank you for sharing, and my deepest sympathies to you all.

—Maryland

I lost my husband on June 17, 2016, to suicide. He also suffered from bipolar disorder. I shared this on my Facebook page because I think so many people need to read this, and perhaps if they do and truly understand what you've laid out, in some small way it might begin to chip away at the stigma of mental illness. I have never understood why people treat those with mental illness differently than people with physical illness. Thank you for your insight. My prayers and thoughts go out to you and your family.

—Anchorage, Alaska

As someone who has almost taken my life many times, my heart goes out to the family of this beautiful, talented young woman. Our system is broken, and it hurts that no matter how hard Kathleen tried, she still struggled. Those medications are not easy to take or tolerate, and she so clearly wanted to get better if she was so diligent about them. We as a society need to understand and do better. May her family find light in God and in continuing to raise awareness for mental health care in Kathleen's name during this dark time.

—Boonton, New Jersey

CHANGED FOREVER

As consoling as all the notes and comments were, Ruth and I will, of course, always dearly miss Katie. Everyone whom I have spoken with who has buried a child has said there will always be a hole in our hearts. The shock has subsided, and we have gotten back to working and enjoying life, but we are forever changed.

The death of a child, especially by suicide, puts a tremendous strain and burden on a marriage. Depression, loneliness, and perhaps anger move in. All too often it leads to divorce. Ruth and I are fortunate that our marriage has endured, but it has changed. Grief is now a part of our marriage. Ruth and I grieve differently, but we can grieve together. We were bound together in a thousand ways, but now we are also bound together in Katie's death. In a mysterious way, the grace of the Holy Spirit that is part of the Sacrament of Matrimony has carried us in our grief.

At times our grief felt almost unbearable. Although its intensity has diminished with time, it has not gone away. We still think about Katie and her death every day. Everyone I have spoken to who has lost a child says the same. The grief that comes with losing a child is different from what comes with other losses. It is intense, and it is long lasting; perhaps it is forever. We need to pray for those who are living with the death of a child, and we need to pray for marriages that face this grief.

FINDING KATIE

From time to time I visit Katie's grave to grieve. There is a simple stone with a cross and her favorite saying engraved on it: "Be Awesome." But I know I will not find Katie at her grave. I know Katie is with the Risen Christ.

As the angels said on the morning of the Resurrection, "Why do you seek the living one among the dead? He is not here, but he has been raised" (Lk 24:5–6). Christ is not dead but lives eternally. A fundamental truth of our faith is that Christ is in us and in everyone we encounter. Therefore, I will find Christ among the living, and where I find Christ is also where I will find Katie because Katie is with the Risen Christ. Both are among the living.[9]

We can find our loved ones in the things that they loved and in the things they struggled with, just as we can find Christ in our own loves and struggles. Katie loved to be around people, yet she struggled with mental illness and died by suicide. So, I find Katie not by grieving alone but by being around people and serving those who struggle with mental illness. In a special way, I see Christ in people who grieve a loved one who died by suicide.

Death is not the final word; even the tragedy of death by suicide is not the final word. The Word of God overcomes death and transforms it to new life. We can participate in this new life by seeing in the death of our loved ones an inspiration to build up the kingdom of God. We overcome the death of a loved one by taking what they loved and bringing that love to the world. We can take the suffering of our lives and transform it into loving service to others who suffer with what they suffered.

Key Points

- Mental illness is an illness, not a character flaw or a moral failing.
- We must see people who live with a mental illness as beautiful creations of God and not define them by the illness.
- Because of stigma and how we treat mental illness, the people who suffer from mental illness needlessly suffer further.
- The medical care for mental illness is not adequate and needs to be significantly improved.
- The death of a child, especially by suicide, puts great strains on a family and on marriages.
- God can transform even the evil of suicide and turn it to help others.

Prayers for the Way

After praying one or more of these simple prayers, sit in silence and contemplate God's presence. Open your heart and mind to God's peace.

God our Father,
I know that all things work for the good
of those who love you,
and that we are called according to your purpose.
Help me to transform my suffering to good
and to your holy purpose. Amen.

Lord Jesus,
During your earthly life illnesses such as leprosy and
blindness were thought to be as signs of moral failure.
Help people today understand that mental illness is
an illness, not a moral failure
or character flaw. Amen.

Holy Spirit,
Help me to remember what my loved one loved
and to bring that love into the Church and the world.
Help me take her [his] suffering and transform it
into loving service for those who still suffer. Amen.

Mother Mary,
Be with couples whose are struggling
because of the tremendous strain and sorrow
that suicide has placed on their marriages.
Help them to bear each other's burdens
and keep holy their covenant of love. Amen.

4.

Praying after a Suicide Loss

Leticia Adams
Catholic Writer and Speaker, Austin, Texas

My son Anthony died from suicide in 2017. He was twenty-two years old and had an entire life ahead of him. My idea of God, Catholicism, and everything associated with it was changed that day. I cursed God, I cried to God, I questioned God. But now I know that God walked beside me the whole time and that he loves Anthony more than I did then or do now. Let me tell you my story—the story of a mom whose son died by suicide and how through the sacraments I was able to pray again and find consolation and hope.

DETERMINED TO BE A "GOOD" CATHOLIC

I converted to Catholicism in 2010 after a life of "looking for love in all the wrong places," as the song goes. That was a reaction to childhood trauma, which included being sexually abused. I came to

41

a parish with a brand-new priest, a great pastor, and a RCIA director who not only understood the teachings of the Catholic Church but also knew Jesus. At this parish I found the one place where all my questions were answered, without freaking anyone out.

I encountered God on my second night of RCIA in the parking lot of the parish as I sat in my car thinking about the words of our director, Noe Rocha, when he looked at me and said, "God loves you more than you think he does. No matter how far you have gone, he loves you and wants you back." I could not know then that in seven years Noe would be standing in the sanctuary of our parish reading the second reading at my son's funeral following his suicide.

Because I came into the Catholic Church after a crazy life of drinking too much, sleeping around, and being an irresponsible parent, when I was initiated into the Church and then married in the Church, I figured life would be smooth sailing. I went to daily Mass and monthly confession. I was involved in a variety of ministries in my parish. I helped Noe with RCIA and anything else he had going on. I was determined to be a "good" Catholic. This included making sure my children were baptized and that we all went to Mass every Sunday.

My oldest son, Anthony, resisted, especially when he got into his teenage years and into girls. We had some huge arguments. Eventually Anthony was old enough to decide for himself, and he decided to stop going to Mass. He also told me he was no longer a Catholic and instead an atheist.

LIFE HAPPENS

Anthony saved my life when I got pregnant with him in 1993, when I was sixteen years old. He gave me something to live for. He loved me when I didn't love myself, and he was my best friend. It was an honor to be his mother and watch him grow into a wonderful father. A talented artist since he could hold a pencil, Anthony also loved to skate, work out, rent movies, bury his younger brother in the backyard, play video games, and shave his eyebrows to annoy his mother. He was always willing to help anyone he could, however he could. He was respectful, kind, and responsible.

After Anthony broke with Catholicism, the next few years brought some extreme changes, both good and bad. A good swing brought the births of Anthony's two beautiful daughters. But the deaths of a number of close family members took a toll on all of us. For Anthony, the death of my uncle in 2016, when Anthony was twenty-one years old, was particularly difficult because Anthony was very close to my uncle.

In the months following my uncle's death, Anthony had a mental breakdown of some kind. Once, we got him to the doctor in the middle of what we thought was a psychotic episode, which the doctor confirmed, but Anthony refused treatment. When he got home with his friends, he told them that the doctor had said there was nothing wrong with him. This was not true of course.

For the next ten months I prayed in every way I could think of for Anthony. He was not well. He was having delusions, and he was paranoid that people were going to hurt his children. He was a lot to deal with. Even though he had moved out of our house and was living with his fiancée and children in their own apartment, his illness took a toll on all of us as a family.

Anthony had always been someone who could help me with his younger siblings, either by managing behavioral issues or by giving them rides to places they needed to be. Suddenly he was no longer reliable, and his siblings felt as though he was no longer available to them as their big brother. That was extremely difficult for them to understand. Anthony was waking me up at all hours of the night with phone calls because he was worried someone was trying to get into his apartment (all delusions and paranoia). He was upsetting his siblings with his angry outbursts, which was not like him at all. His behavior was chaotic and unpredictable. All these things pointed to him having some mental illness issues, but he would not agree to see a doctor, so there was never a diagnosis. Yet he was also scared by his behavior, and in moments of clarity he would say that he was sorry for being difficult.

Then ten months after my uncle died, his wife died in February 2017. Anthony took the news hard, and I made a point to check in with him a lot. It was also when I began to fear him hurting himself. I have never prayed as much as I prayed for Anthony for those months. I was terrified of something, but I had no idea what that something was going to be. I just knew the possibility was that it would be very bad.

ANTHONY'S GONE

I went to a parish to venerate the relics of St. Anthony of Padua, whom my son was named after. I prayed for God to help my son find his way back to the Church and for Anthony's salvation. I took the prayer card I got and gave it to Anthony. But he was gone just days later. On March 8, 2017, my husband found my son dead in our garage at 4:45 p.m.

The last time I talked to Anthony was at 1:51 p.m. that afternoon when he called me asking if he could use my car when I got back home. Just that morning he told me he wanted to come back to the Church. He wanted to use my car to go talk to our priest at the parish. I told my husband that I thought Anthony was getting better and everything was going to be okay. I was full of hope that he was finally going to come back to me.

When I got home, he was nowhere to be found and I assumed his fiancée had picked him up. Little did I know what was on the other side of the garage wall. It never occurred to me that he would have taken his own life.

Everything that happened after my husband found Anthony went fast but also in slow motion. I walked past the open garage door and could see the outline of my son's body. I first thought of keeping his manner of death to myself because I was scared of what people would think, but with the grace of God I decided that I was not going to ever be ashamed of my son. I would be angry, sad, depressed, and confused, but I would not allow myself to even consider being ashamed.

THE CHURCH PRAYS FOR MY SON'S SOUL

From the minute that we found Anthony, I knew I needed the help of my priests to pray for his soul—not because he took his own life but because praying for the dead is a huge part of our faith. So, my pastor, Fr. Dean, was the first phone call I made after calling 911. He was right behind the ambulance. Fr. Jonathan, the priest who had baptized Anthony and all my kids and had walked with me through my conversion, was right behind Fr. Dean. Fr. Jonathan waited with us until the police allowed us to bless Anthony's body. He had been with me through a lot by this point, but this was by far the hardest thing either one of us had faced.

Anthony had four priests concelebrate his funeral Mass. Fr. Jonathan was so very understanding and considerate. As part of the preparations for Anthony's funeral, he asked me what we would like him to say in the homily. I told him I wanted it to be a testimony of God's love for all of us and that in no way was Anthony's suicide a part of God's plan for his life. Fr. Jonathan did a great job at making those things clear. Because he had been the one to baptize Anthony and bless Anthony's body, the love he had for Anthony came through in his homily, which was a beautiful gift of love for the rest of us.

People from all over the world were praying for my son's soul. Jennifer Fulwiler, who hosts a radio show on the Catholic Channel on Sirius XM radio, spoke about the loss of Anthony to her international audience. Jen's request for prayers for us, along with many other Catholic friends who also requested prayers for Anthony in the days after his suicide, led to an outpouring of love and prayers.

This led to such great love in me for my Church and for all the kind people who make up the Body of Christ. It also made me grateful for the many ways that we as Catholics can offer prayers for people who are suffering, including through the use of social media. People started tagging me in pictures of candles they lit for Anthony all over the place. In the days, months, and year that I could not bring myself to pray, total strangers praying for me kept me connected to God and to Anthony.

In the weeks that followed Anthony's death, many priests who are close to us reached out to help us through that terrible time. One priest blessed the garage. Fr. Jonathan prayed with us as though he was part of our family. Another priest came over and blessed St. Benedict medals to put around our house. We picked St. Benedict medals because I knew that my entire family would need all the help we could get to stay strong in the months and years to come. St. Benedict was a saint who did not fear anything because he trusted God completely.

Another priest, who had been at our parish for a while and was now a pastor of a different parish, helped me through my anger by taking time out of his busy life to have a phone conversation with me. A priest from Canada and a friend of mine through social media had been praying for Anthony in Rome in the days leading up to Anthony's suicide. Added to the prayers of all these priests, who have continued to pray for my family and offer up Masses for Anthony, were the hundreds of Mass cards and perpetual enrollments that began to flood in through the mail.

CUSSING OUT AND QUESTIONING GOD

Despite all this help, for the next year I was very angry. One of the first things I did was go to Mass and kneel in front of the tabernacle, cussing out God. Then I stopped going to Mass, I stopped praying, and I strongly considered leaving Catholicism altogether. I had prayed so hard for my son, and God just sat there and watched as he took his own life. Things went wrong all the time, and this was one time that it would have been helpful for something to break, like the beam or the rope that my son hanged himself with, so that my son's life could be saved. But it didn't!

I saw a news story shortly after Anthony's suicide where a boy was saved from a fast-moving current. His mother was on the news and said, "God must have a purpose for his life to have saved him," and I threw a glass at the television. If that were true, if God had saved that boy because he had a purpose for that kid's life, then did God not have a purpose for my son's life? How do we explain that? How do we say "thank God" when someone's kid does not die when other people's sons are dying? What is the point of praying if God was just going to let people kill themselves anyway?

I also questioned whether I had prayed the right way. I have heard of miracles where God brings children back to life after they have been dead for a while, and that made me wonder about my son. Was his life not worth it?

For the first year after Anthony's suicide, I had a hard time praying at all, other than to tell God that his plan sucked and that I hated it. I cried for my son, and I hoped he was in heaven. But I also wondered, if that was the way to heaven, why should any of us not follow in his footsteps? I went into a deep depression. I truly believe now that what kept me alive were the prayers of everyone who loved me and my family.

That first year was extremely difficult for me. Our priests, friends, and my therapist have stood with me in the darkest grief. I had my own mental health issues going on, and fortunately I was seeing a therapist to help me with my grief. In the midst of this, my grandbaby was having panic attacks, my husband was struggling silently, and my other kids were having nightmares and other troubling issues. We were all devastated, and I was so very angry with God.

SLOWLY CAME HEALING AND THE RETURN OF HOPE

Eventually, though, I began to see that making peace with God was the only way I was going to survive. I began to pray a little here and there after the first anniversary of Anthony's suicide. Slowly I started going back to Mass. At first I was just sitting there seething with rage, but eventually I was able to pay attention during Mass and listen to what God was saying to me.

It was at Mass that I was able to lay my heart out in the open. It was where I could talk to God about how broken I was and ask him to heal me. At daily Mass I sat in front of a painting of St. Rafael, where he is saying, "Before long, God will heal you," and I kept begging God for that moment. I began to read the daily readings and to keep a journal. I continue those spiritual disciplines and read the Bible regularly. These practices help me to feel stronger and stronger.

It was more than two years after we found Anthony dead in the garage before I finally felt as if God had, in fact, healed me just a little. Now I can breathe. I can pray. I can go to Mass and feel the grace of God. It is still not perfect, but I know that God loves me. I know that God loves Anthony.

The grief is still there, and it is just as painful, if not more painful, the further I get from having last seen my son alive. It is still difficult for me to watch videos of Anthony and to hear his voice. I see his children growing up knowing they will not know him.

But even with all that, I have hope again—hope that I can tell Anthony's story. I will let people know that suicide is something we all must face as a society for the sake of our children. I have hope that I can be happy and not forget my son or leave him behind. And more than anything, I have begun to do the things I enjoy doing and live my life.

LETTING GOD INTO OUR SUFFERING

Our Catholic faith shines in the darkness. Our Catholic faith helps us endure the grief and suffering. We talk about suffering so much. We pray the Stations of the Cross to remember Christ's suffering. The saints have written volumes on how to allow God into our suffering so that it is redeemed. Reading their writings consoled me and helped me to let God into my suffering.

Through prayer I was able to see light when it was nowhere to be found. I would not have ever gotten to this place without my faith. Never.

Key Points

- Suicide happens even in the families of "good" Catholics.
- The priests were with the family immediately after the suicide and worked with the family on what they hoped for in the funeral.
- Prayers of the Church community helped to console the family.
- Ongoing prayers and rituals help the family grieve.
- Suicide and the death of a child changes a person's relationship with God.
- We can find healing and live in hope after a suicide.

Prayers for the Way

After praying one or more of these simple prayers, sit in silence and contemplate God's presence. Open your heart and mind to God's peace.

> God our Father,
> I am often angry and I cry with the psalmist,
> *Why do you forget me? Why must I go about mourning?*
> (Ps 42:10).
> I give my anger to you as the only prayer I can offer.
> Amen.

> Lord Jesus,
> You minister to us through your priests.
> Help them be a healing presence in my life
> and in the lives of all who are grieving the suicide of a
> loved one. Amen.

> Holy Spirit,
> Help me see your presence in the Church,
> in my parish community,
> and in all those who have sought to console me. Amen.

> Mother Mary,
> You accepted the death of your Son.
> Show me how to accept this suicide and be healed.
> Amen.

5.

What Leads a Person to Suicide?

David A. Jobes, PhD, ABPP, with Deacon Ed Shoener

What leads a person to die by suicide? That question is at the heart of my medical research. I am the director of the Suicide Prevention Lab at the Catholic University of America. I have been at this work for more than thirty-five years, and the focus of my research, clinical practice, and research is broadly centered on understanding suicidal risk, preventing it, and lowering its position as a leading cause of death.

Suicide is a worldwide public health challenge. No population, culture, faith tradition, or subgroup is immune to its scourge, which ranks among the most tragic of human events. A staggering 10.6 million American adults have serious suicidal thoughts each year, while 1.4 million will attempt to take their life. More than forty-seven thousand people across all age groups in the United States died by suicide in 2017, and suicide is the tenth leading cause of death in our country.[10]

While suicide rates in the United States go up and down, when we look at the big picture we see the persistence of the problem. For example, in 1914, the rate was 16 per 100,000 people, and the rate in 2018 is about the same. Many of us who study suicide and its causes began to think we had turned a corner in the 1990s when rates started to decline and were as low as 10.5 per 100,000 in 1999.[11] But we have seen a discouraging and gradual increase over the last twenty years, with rates rising back up to the range of 16 per 100,000 people. These data are worrisome, especially in regard to suicide rates for young children, teenagers, veterans, and active duty armed services members. We had thought that the rates came down in the eighties and nineties because of our innovative suicide prevention work and research, but the data suggest that there are still challenges we face with this public health problem.

No one really knows why the rates have gone back up. Anyone who claims to know is merely speculating. In the past we have found some connections between suicide rates and the economy and unemployment, but this association does not account for recent rates. There is a lot of speculation about the impact of social media and disconnection and loss of faith, but these arguments have not been proven. Bottom line, no one really knows why the suicide rates have crept back up, but they are obviously concerning.

THE NATURE OF PSYCHOLOGICAL PAIN

The nature of psychological pain at the heart of suicidal states is fundamentally different than physical pain. Dr. Ed Shneidman, a psychologist who was at UCLA, called it "psychache." He created a word for it to make sure it was understood as different from depression, anxiety, or existential angst. Psychache is an exquisite suffering of the mind that is so unbearable that in the mind's eye of the suffering person, the only way it can be extinguished is through death.

Shneidman wrote, "Psychache refers to the hurt, anguish, soreness, aching, psychological pain in the psyche, the mind. It is intrinsically psychological—the pain of excessively felt shame, or guilt, or humiliation, or whatever. When it occurs, its reality is introspectively undeniable. Suicide occurs when the psychache is deemed by that person to be unbearable. This means that suicide also has to do with different individual thresholds for enduring psychological pain."[12]

The *Catechism of the Catholic Church* lists "grave psychological disturbances, anguish, a great fear of hardship, suffering or torture" (2242) as factors that can diminish the responsibility of a person who dies by suicide. All of these can manifest in a form of psychological pain. Most suicidal people feel tortured and oftentimes have little remission from their suffering. What ultimately compels someone to end their life is thus an unbearable degree of angst and intense and pervasive psychological suffering that is fundamentally linked to the idea that the *only* way I can end this unbearable suffering is through suicide.

THE LIMITS OF CURRENT ASSESSMENT AND TREATMENT METHODS

Despite hard-earned progress in the field of suicide prevention, still far too many lives are touched by the tragedy of suicide. So it's important for you to know about the specialization of suicide "postvention." As someone who has lost a loved one to suicide, there are many resources available to you, for example, through the American

Association of Suicidology (www.suicidology.org), the American Foundation for Suicide Prevention (www.afsp.org), and the Suicide Prevention Resource Center (www.sprc.org).

Those of you who have lost someone dear to suicide are often loaded with guilt, wondering if you could have done something. I understand. I think about my faculty colleague years ago who was literally across the hall from me. I think about the day when he stopped by my office door and lingered after some small talk, but I turned back to my computer. I regret not having talked to him that day, because a few days later he took his life. While I do not think I caused his suicide, given what happened I really wished I had talked to him that day.

More recently we had a child in our neighborhood who jumped off an overpass onto a very busy highway to his death. I know his parents did everything they could do. He was hospitalized three times and took lots of different medications. And they knew me, we were family friends, and our older sons were friends. And we too wonder, *If only we had . . .*

Such is the nature of suicidal loss—so many questions, so many missed opportunities, and so many regrets for things that might have been done *in hindsight*. Such musings can be quite painful, and obviously no amount of hindsight will ever bring back your precious person. As a survivor, you are thrust into a club that no one wants to join.

FINDING GOD'S GRACE AND HEALING

No family, faith, or demographic is immune to the impact of suicide. As Catholics we may wonder how God can abide the deaths of our loved ones by their own hands. The unanswerable questions surrounding a suicide invariably haunt anyone who loses someone to it. While we may never have answers to all the painful questions, we must do all we can do to reduce suicide-related suffering—in all its forms.

I know a couple that lost their beloved daughter to suicide. As highly educated professionals and loving parents they did everything they knew to do to save their daughter. Their daughter was repeatedly hospitalized and took many different medications through the years. Since their daughter's death I've been journeying with them to figure out how they can use their financial resources to have the biggest impact to prevent other suicides. I have so much admiration for what they are trying to do. Every time we have one of these discussions, they lose their daughter once again. Still, they continue to turn their private tragedy into something productive and healing so that, if possible, other people do not have to go through what they have.

As a clinician, the question I always pose to my patients who are grieving a death by suicide is, "How can you honor this person's memory?" I tell them that the best thing they can do is honor the memories and live as they would have you live. And that, to me, is the best advice I can give: to carry on as this person you lost would want you to live. I also gently suggest that your loved one should be remembered by how they lived, not by how they died. I believe there is grace within these therapeutic efforts. But after many years of working in this field I have come to know that with suicide loss there can be a unique form of grief that never ends, yet the pain certainly lessens in time. And many of those with whom I work find unexpected gifts in their pain and grief. These gifts are often shared with others and therein lies God's tend mercy and infinite love.

Key Points

- No one really knows why suicide rates have gone back up to historic averages. Anybody who says they do know why rates have been increasing is merely speculating.
- Suicide has to do with different individual thresholds for enduring psychological pain.
- Despite hard-earned progress, far too many lives are still touched by the tragedy of suicide. We can do a lot, but that does not guarantee suicides will not occur.
- No family, faith, or demographic is immune to the impact of suicide.

Prayers for the Way

After praying one or more of these simple prayers, sit in silence and contemplate God's presence. Open your heart and mind to God's peace.

> God our Father,
> You know all things, and I do not.
> Help me to accept the reality that I may never fully
> understand why my loved one died by suicide. Amen.

Lord Jesus,
You suffered intensely on the Cross and cried out,
My God, my God why have you abandoned me?
My loved one must have had such intense,
persistent psychological pain.
Remove his [her] suffering and bring him [her] eternal
peace. Amen.

Holy Spirit,
You are the source of all wisdom.
Give wisdom and strength to medical professionals
who treat those with a mental illness or who are suicidal.
Amen.

Mother Mary,
You always honor the memory of your son.
Guide me to find ways to honor my loved one's memory
and to live gratefully and as he [she] would have hoped.
Amen.

6.

What the Catholic Church Teaches about Suicide

Bishop John Dolan and Deacon Ed Shoener

The Church cannot make the pain, grief, and suffering of losing a loved one to suicide go away. That is not within its power. But the Church can help bring the light of Christ into the darkness of suicide loss, and the Holy Spirit will pour the healing balm of Christ's love upon the wounds of those of us who are grieving. This spiritual healing is contained, in part, within the teachings of Christ's Church. His mercy flows through these teachings, which offer hope in the compassion and love of Christ who calls us to himself. Christ is the Divine Physician who can heal our every wound.

Our own faith may be challenged by the awful circumstances of suicide. These challenges may come as we ask questions such as the following:

- How will my loved one be judged by God?
- Is my loved one in hell?
- Will they be punished in purgatory?

- Is it possible for my loved one to go to heaven?
- Can I pray for my loved one who died by suicide?
- Can my loved one who died by suicide pray for me?

Questions about death and the afterlife are a part of being human. It is helpful to remember some key teachings of the Church on death, judgment, purgatory, heaven, and hell.

A REVIEW OF THE FOUR LAST THINGS

Our faith tradition considers four last things when we close our eyes to this life: death, judgment, heaven, and hell. According to the *Catechism of the Catholic Church*, "Each man receives his eternal retribution in his immortal soul at the very moment of his death, in a particular judgment that refers his life to Christ: either entrance into the blessedness of Heaven—through purification—or immediate and everlasting damnation" (1022).

Regarding purification, the Church's teaching on purgatory is presented very briefly in the *Catechism*. "All who die in God's grace and friendship, but still imperfectly purified, are indeed assured of their eternal salvation; but after death they undergo purification, so as to achieve the holiness necessary to enter the joy of heaven" (1030).

PRAYING FOR ALL SOULS

Although the Church does not teach that there is universal salvation, the Church expects the faithful to pray as if all can be saved. The Fatima prayer for Jesus to "lead all souls into heaven, especially those in most need of thy mercy," or the St. Faustina's Divine Mercy request that Jesus atone for "our sins and those of the whole world," are just a few examples of our response to the Lord who himself prayed "that they may all be one" (Jn 17:21).

When a loved one dies by suicide, we wonder how we can still show them that we love them. Simply, we pray for them.

As we celebrate a Mass or obtain indulgences on their behalf "through works of mercy and charity and by acts of penance," we offer up the burden of suffering for those who have gone before us (*CCC*, 1032).

The Church's teaching on purgatory is beautiful and can even be healing for survivors as we pray together for those who have died by suicide. Reciting the following prayer offered at funerals is healing for both the deceased and their survivors:

> Eternal Rest grant unto them O Lord. And let perpet
>   ual light
>   shine upon them.
> May they rest in peace. Amen.
> May their soul and the souls of all the faithful departed
>   through the mercy of God, rest in peace. Amen.

In turn, we trust that those who have gone before us, including those in purgatory, continue to pray for us.

Those in the state of purification are in communion with us who live in this world and with those who enjoy eternal beatitude in the fullness of heaven. *Lumen Gentium* expresses this perfectly:

> Until the Lord shall come in His majesty, and all the angels with Him and death being destroyed, all things are subject to Him, some of His disciples are exiles on earth, some having died are purified, and others are in glory beholding "clearly God Himself triune and one, as He is but all in various ways and degrees are in communion in the same charity of God and neighbor and all sing the same hymn of glory to our God." (49)

JUDGMENT

The nature of purgatory, heaven, and hell are not nearly as important for us as the questions of how we will be judged and who will do the judging. As Catholics, the answer is simple. All of humanity will, in a particular and then universal way, stand before the judgment seat of Christ who is our Judge. Matthew 25 gives us a glimpse of the judge who will separate us, as a shepherd separates sheep from goats.

If we live and die faithfully and lovingly in Christ, we have a moral assurance that we will be judged mercifully and that heaven will be our reward. If we refuse to live faithfully and lovingly in Christ, scripture refers to those who will be judged harshly and will be found in hell. There is simply death, judgment, hell, or purgatory and heaven.

What is not found in the *Catechism*, in sacred scripture, or in the tradition of the Church is permission for us to usurp the role of Christ Jesus and become the judge of the dead. This belongs to Christ and the mercy of God alone.

Mercy is generously poured out upon all of humanity because we are a sinful people. We are a people who live in a realm of concupiscence, and being forever tempted, we are apt to sin.

Our faith teaches that from the moment sin entered the world, God began a plan of redemption. "Oh happy fault! Oh necessary sin of Adam, which gained for us so great a redeemer" (from the *Exsultet* at the Easter Vigil). Covenant after covenant, from Adam through Noah, Abraham, Moses, King David, the Prophets, and Christ Jesus, God revealed his mercy. Gratefully, God's mercy is unmerited.

Scattered through the pages of history, human beings showed glimpses of true virtue and fidelity. Of course, the same pages show a human world of vice and downright evil. We are physical beings with souls of intellect and free will who were made in the image and likeness of God. This is a starting point for understanding our uniqueness in all of God's visible and invisible creation. Yet, we are tempted and inclined to sin (concupiscence); we willfully succumb to sin and veer away from the will of God. Our conscience, on the other hand, urges us to remain with God and to live virtuous lives. On a very basic level, this "doctrine of humanity" is the Church's teaching of our human condition.

However, a development of the doctrine on the dignity of the human person acknowledges concupiscence as something more than just a rational or willful choosing of vice versus virtue. An understanding of the doctrine of the human person must recall this reality that the sciences of psychology and psychiatry continue to provide. Whether through chemical, biological, or situational realities (post-trauma, childhood abuse, drug dependent homes, and so on), many of us do not in fact freely and willfully choose to abandon God or human virtues. Due to these situations there is some lack of culpability or blameworthiness. In the case of those who have died through suicide, this understanding of our human nature must always be considered.

You may have noticed that the phrase "committed suicide" is not used in this book. Rather we, and most mental health advocates, use phrases such as "died by suicide" or "took their life." Using such phrases more accurately reflects Church teaching by naming the action without indicating that the commission of personal sin necessarily occurred. We don't pass judgement, leaving that to God alone as the Church teaches us to do. This slight change in language can make a huge difference in how we talk about suicide. We shift from judgement to a healthier discussion on mental illness and the real causes of suicide, which may in the long run help lead to better treatment programs and a reduction in the rate of suicide.

A COMPASSIONATE PASTORAL RESPONSE TO SUICIDE

In 2018, the bishops of California issued a pastoral letter on caring for those who suffer from mental illness titled, *Hope and Healing*. The letter took an in-depth look at the spiritual and pastoral issues surrounding mental illness, as well as suicide. The letter was widely praised and described as "the new standard for mental health ministries around the world."

In their pastoral letter, the bishops addressed the issue of suicide, which is all too often associated with mental illness. The letter provides authoritative pastoral guidance to Catholic leaders on the attitude that ministers should have when they minister to people who are grieving a suicide. The bishops addressed "the heartbreaking tragedy of suicide" and said that "those who have lost loved ones to suicide . . . suffer especially painful wounds and are particularly in need of our compassion and support."

> Those who lose a loved one to suicide need particular care and attention, often for considerable periods of time. They have not only lost someone dear to them and are deeply grieving, their intense grief is often complicated by feelings of shame, confusion, anger or guilt. They may replay in their minds their last conversation with the loved one and wonder whether they could have done more to prevent the tragic death. Furthermore, they often feel alone and misunderstood, as though they cannot discuss this with anyone. Catholics must convey to them that we are not afraid to open this difficult conversation, that they need not feel ashamed to discuss their profound anguish and loss. While healing in these situations happens only very slowly, we must be willing to walk this long road with suicide survivors, to help console them with our unconditional friendship and with sensitive pastoral care.
>
> Let us remember that Christ's heart—a heart both human and divine—is merciful beyond measure. It is here that we place our hope. It is into Christ's hands stretched out on the cross that we entrust our loved ones who are suffering and all who have died as a result of a mental illness. We pray that the departed may find God's peace, a peace that surpasses all understanding. We pray that the angels will one day welcome them to that place where their grief will be extinguished, where they will suffer no more.

CHRIST'S JUDGMENT AND MERCY

If, as the California bishops proclaimed, God's mercy is "beyond measure," then we must approach suicide with mercy as well.

As we consider the act of suicide, we must remember that that one act cannot define the level of fidelity in our loved one's lives. There are many charitable, loving, and faithful souls who are also lost in a world of psychological oppression. It is our prayer that God judges our loved one not by a singular act but rather on their general and fundamental stance in life.

Whether or not the person who jumps from a bridge cries out at the last moment to God for mercy, God understands the nature of that person. It would be rare that a person who died by suicide did so by acting with his or her full use of intellect and free will. It is also an oversimplification to assume that a suicidal person has a lack of faith in God. The development of the doctrine on the dignity of the human person allows the science of psychology and psychiatry to weigh in on each person's level of culpability, even while that person seeks a right relationship with his or her Creator and Redeemer.

This isn't to say that we aren't called to be virtuous people. Christianity demands a carrying of the cross daily, an exercise of faith, and a life of charity. However, simply put, some people, due to their psychological makeup, life circumstance, and other factors, are more equipped to be virtuous than others.

Suicide is clearly different from death through natural or accidental causes. The Church will forever say it is never right to end one's own life. The act of suicide, in and of itself, is a grave matter. The act, however, is one thing; the intention and the circumstances that lead up to that act is another. When a person who has bipolar disorder or schizophrenia, or is posttraumatically disordered, ends their own life, it is assumed they were not of the right mind to willfully act against our common and basic human instinct to live. This does not dismiss the gravity of the act itself. In fact, it is sinful in that it "misses the mark" (Greek expression for sin) of what it means to live and love happily with God, with others, and with oneself. But it certainly puts things into perspective if we are inclined to pass judgment on suicidal persons.

CHURCH TEACHING ON SUICIDE

Up into the last century it was the practice of the Church to deny a funeral Mass to people who died by suicide and to not allow them to be buried in a Catholic cemetery. Fortunately, as our understanding of mental illness and psychology has improved, the Church has developed a more nuanced and compassionate teaching on suicide. Now, the Church's teaching seeks to reassure those who grieve a loved one who died by suicide that the Church prays for those who have died by suicide.

The *Catechism of the Catholic Church* was updated in 1992 by Pope John Paul II. The teaching on suicide is short and to the point.

> Everyone is responsible for his life before God who has given it to him. It is God who remains the sovereign Master of life. We are obliged to accept life gratefully and preserve it for his honor and the salvation of our souls. We are stewards, not owners, of the life God has entrusted to us. It is not ours to dispose of. (2280)

Suicide contradicts the natural inclination of the human being to preserve and perpetuate his life. It is gravely contrary to the just love of self. It likewise offends love of neighbor because it unjustly breaks the ties of solidarity with family, nation, and other human societies to which we continue to have obligations. Suicide is contrary to love for the living God. (2281)

If suicide is committed with the intention of setting an example, especially to the young, it also takes on the gravity of scandal. Voluntary co-operation in suicide is contrary to the moral law. Grave psychological disturbances, anguish, or grave fear of hardship, suffering, or torture can diminish the responsibility of the one committing suicide. (2282)

We should not despair of the eternal salvation of persons who have taken their own lives. By ways known to him alone, God can provide the opportunity for salutary repentance. The Church prays for persons who have taken their own lives. (2283)

We have talked to many people who have attempted suicide. Everyone was glad they survived the suicide attempt and agrees with the essential teaching the first two paragraphs (2280 and 2281): suicide is wrong. However, they also agree with the third paragraph (2282): their suicide attempt was driven by irrational thoughts and psychological disorders.

The final paragraph (2283) has brought great comfort to us and to many others who grieve the loss of loved one by suicide. We do not despair for the eternal salvation of our loved ones. We know they are loved by God, and we look to Mary and the saints for consolation and help.

Key Points

- Christ's mercy flows through the teachings of the Church. These teachings can help heal those who are grieving a suicide with the promise of the resurrection.
- Purification can be found in purgatory. Christ will offer his mercy to purify a person of all that led to their death by suicide. We need to pray for the souls in purgatory.
- Pope Francis said about those who have died by suicide, "To the very end, to the very end, there is the mercy of God."
- We should not despair of the eternal salvation of persons who have taken their own lives. The Church prays for those who have died by suicide.

Prayers for the Way

After praying one or more of these simple prayers, sit in silence and contemplate God's presence. Open your heart and mind to God's peace.

> God our Father,
> You did not create my loved one to die by suicide.
> You created her [him] to live with you for all eternity.
> Help me not despair of eternal salvation for [name].
> Give me hope and confidence in your loving mercy.
> Amen.

> Lord Jesus,
> You sit at the right hand of the Father
> to judge the living and the dead.
> Grant mercy to[name], purify him [her],
> and give him [her] entrance into the joy of heaven.
> Amen.

Holy Spirit,
Be with your Church and its leaders,
as they guide your people with teaching
about mental illness and suicide
and the pastoral care both require. Amen.

Mother Mary, our advocate and helper,
intercede for [name]
and carry her [him] toward the gifts of eternal salvation.
Amen.

7.

Posttraumatic Growth after Suicide

Melinda Moore, PhD

Department of Psychology, Eastern Kentucky University

> All death unsettles us, but suicide leaves us with a very particular series of emotional, moral, and religious scars. It brings with it an ache, a chaos, a darkness, and a stigma that has to be experienced to be believed. Sometimes we deny it, but it's always there irrespective of our religious and moral beliefs.
>
> —Fr. Ron Rolheiser

Suicide, perhaps more than any other cause of death, challenges our ways of thinking about who has died and our relationship to them. Inevitably, existential and religious questions arise for those of us who are the surviving loved ones, the suicide loss survivors or "suicide bereaved," as we struggle with our relationship to God and try to navigate this traumatic loss within the context of our practice of faith.

I WAS GIVEN PERMISSION TO TALK ABOUT MY GRIEF

After the suicide of my husband, Conor, I recall sitting with a compassionate stranger, Fr. Bill Maroon, a priest to whom I had been referred by one of his parishioners in Columbus, Ohio. I was a new Catholic, having converted and entered the Church the year before my husband's death. I was uncertain how to make sense of my new faith in the context of the most painful, most perplexing event of my life. *Why did this happen to me? Why did this happen to Conor?* Other clergy with whom I had come in contact had been unable to answer my questions as to how to assimilate this experience into my journey of faith.

Fr. Maroon sat and cried with me, recounting—really reteaching in a profound way—stories of the Old Testament prophet Job and how he coped with enormous grief and his questions about where God was in the midst of suffering. *Where was God in this?* In that moment of intense pain, I was given permission to question, like Job, God's whereabouts, to sink deeply into my disappointment and grief. Fr. Maroon gave me permission, not by telling me, but by doing, by crying with me, by being present to my intense pain, and by re-storying. Through Fr. Maroon's fearless compassion and retelling of Job's story, I was reminded how close our experiences are to those in the Bible and how real God's mercy is for our loved ones and us. I will never forget this godly man: how healing his ministry of aftercare was for me and how it allowed me to begin the task of reshaping my grief.

WHAT WILL PEOPLE SAY?

Because Conor was Irish and came to the United States to study at Ohio State University, I wanted to participate in an Irish tradition of the "Month's Mind Mass," a mass that occurs one month after someone dies as a way of celebrating the deceased's life of faith and commending them to the Lord. I thought this would be an opportunity to invite his friends and colleagues at Ohio State to participate in a memorial ceremony because they were unable to attend his funeral and burial in Ireland.

I was in unchartered territory and was uncertain what the priest would say about the disposition of Conor's soul during the Mass. I was certain that his soul was with God, but my own friends' and family's reaction to his suicide, not to mention my community newspaper's (Conor's suicide was reported in our local newspaper) and my work colleagues' apparent horror, communicated something different. Even a local priest, a friend of Conor's father, told me that he was not "certain of the disposition of Conor's soul," in response to my question about my own walk of faith. It was as if Conor's act of self-destruction clouded ministering to my own need for clarity about his death. I was certain that people who surrounded me weren't sure about the disposition of his soul. This made the experience of celebrating Conor's life of faith in the Catholic Church— much less "commending him to the Lord"—uncomfortable.

I was also nervous because I knew the priests of St. Patrick's Church, a church supported by the Dominican Order, were a more traditional, conservative order, especially Fr. Stephen Hayes, the American-born, Gaelic-speaking lawyer/priest who would preside at this Mass. I was nervous but tried to stay obedient in my heart, trusting that Fr. Hayes would handle things well, even if it caused pain and discomfort in my own heart. When Fr. Hayes entered the church and began the service, he spoke with direction and clarity, asserting that Conor's soul was with God by virtue of his Baptism. *Conor was with God.* All questions were vanquished, all doubt erased, and all misrepresented Church teaching redirected. There seemed to be a sigh of relief among the attendees, as if they too feared condemnation. Fr. Hayes showed leadership, compassion, and a profound understanding in his very first utterance. I will never forget that moment and how it provided enormous comfort in my time of greatest pain, and buoyed my own faith practice, even all these years later.

In this moment, I was able to love, honor, and celebrate Conor, which I have done and learned to do over and over again, in spite of how he died. I can now honestly say *in spite* of how he died, although it was something I would never have dared utter at the time.

At the time, in my work in public health (I worked for the Ohio Department of Health), in my practice of faith, and among my social groups, the message I received from others about how to react to his death was one of silence. It was a silence that stank of shame. I participated in the taint of his death by being his wife. I *should* have cared for him better. I *should* have protected him, even from himself. I *should* be *ashamed* as well.

My coworkers were uncomfortable around me, to the point of ignoring me or remaining silent on my experience of loss. I went into meetings with my boss, the director of the Ohio Department of Health, and was never extended condolences, only questions about where my work was during the week I left to bury my husband in Ireland. The assistant director did extend condolences, although he did so uncomfortably, with great difficulty and caution with the words he chose.

My family came to my rescue at the time of Conor's death and then went strangely silent as I tried to process this loss, acknowledge his presence, within the context of family functions and holidays. I did not blame any of them. What he did was horrendous, and it happened to all of us, not just me. Still, none of us understood it. I was desperately trying to do so, thinking that if I had some understanding, then I might have some peace.

MY SEARCH TO UNDERSTAND SUICIDE

At the time of his death, the science around suicide was very much in the Dark Ages, although Dr. Edwin Shneidman had already founded the study of suicidology in the 1950s and the American Association of Suicidology in the 1960s. I was working in public health in Ohio, and my work addressed every behavior-related cause of morbidity and mortality, including smoking cessation, low birth weight babies, and even mental health issues, except we were not talking about suicide. Still, 1,200 Ohioans were killing themselves every year. No one was talking about it. It was like these people never existed or even mattered.

In the year after his death, I scoured bookstores and every resource I could think of to understand Conor's death. One day, in the downtown Cathedral bookstore, I found a book by Adina Wrobleski, *Suicide Survivors: A Guide for Those Left Behind*. Adina lost her stepdaughter to suicide in 1979. Despite searching endlessly for information, resources, and support to help her and her family through the tragedy, Adina was unable to find what she needed. She immersed herself in mental health research, hoping to learn everything she could about suicide and its causes. Adina quickly became an expert, speaking and writing publicly about the topic. By the late 1980s, she became nationally known, taking part in research and writing journal articles and books.

I reached out to Adina after I devoured her book. She was not a scientist but wrote in plain English for a broad range of readers. She wrote about the feelings of guilt and shame that so many suicide survivors felt. I didn't even know the term *suicide survivor* but intuitively knew that was exactly what I was. I survived something cataclysmic, like my own private earthquake, shattering and destroying my life, my very being, as I knew it.

When I spoke to Adina on the phone in 1996, I remember feeling I had been thrown a lifeline in this disaster. She was a first responder. She consoled and informed me, patched me up, so I could keep on going. I don't remember much of our conversation, but I do remember feeling I was met with an otherworldly compassion, someone who felt my own pain and despair deeply. I didn't know how I was going to survive this experience, but I knew she had inspired hope in me that I could, somehow, someway, do the same.

For several years, I just took care of myself. I continued working in public health, took post-baccalaureate classes at Ohio State University, putting one foot in front of the other, but not really knowing where my journey was taking me. Previously, I had frenetically planned and meticulously scheduled, working full time and going to school full time. I had a career trajectory and a path squared away. After Conor's death, I had to collapse into a slower, intentional way of life. I attended Mass and grew deeper in my faith and closer to God too as I trusted him to carry me, a solitary, isolated being, unsure that I would survive but trusting that *thy will be done.*

SUFFERING AND MY SPIRITUAL LIFE

I sunk into the writings and teaching of Mother Teresa on suffering. I could not understand why God allowed this to happen to Conor or to me. Conor's mother had suffered her entire life, and she did not deserve this fate. I could not understand, but Mother Teresa made my suffering nearly palatable. So did Thomas Merton; his love for the pleasures of the secular world and his desire to be united by God amused and befriended me. Therese of Lisieux and other mystics helped me understand the spiritual union, in pain, with God.

Tonglen meditation was something I learned through the videos of the Buddhist nun Pema Chodron. Her book *When Things Fall Apart* helped me believe that this place of despair and collapse was also a place of creation. Various kinds of meditation allow us to consciously take suffering and accept it; to transform our suffering into peace, joy, and love; and to find healing, release, relaxation, and well-being. I practiced Tonglen meditation to lovingly connect with all the other "suicide survivors" in the world whom I was traveling with, at a distance; we never knew each other but were connected by an experience so profound and painful that we could not help but know, on a spiritual level, that we were there, suffering together, and trusting that our loved ones were safely in God's arms.

Yet, my spiritual pursuits did not satisfy the obsession I had with Conor's death, the gigantic *why* of his death: *why did he turn on himself*, and *how could God allow him to do it*? It did not stop the desperation and the hurt, the unending emotional ache, and the physical pain in my chest. It did, however, provide a salve to my agony.

Kneeling at the altar for communion every Sunday, I took the Eucharist and looked up at the fallen Christ and visualized marrying my pain with his. That act was all I had and I knew it. This was it. This was a practice. I did it every Sunday and began to do it in my own prayer at home. I suffered with Christ on the Cross and, in so doing, experienced a grace, a transcendence of pain, and a healing presence that transformed me. The simultaneous feeling of profound love for all living beings and my own sense of personal strength, while at the same time continuing to suffer and grieve, was a place I will never forget. As I knelt at the altar in St. Patrick's Church in Columbus, Ohio, I knew I would never be the same again.

LEARNING HOW TO BE A SUICIDE SURVIVOR

My heart, my entire being, had been broken open in a way that had never been touched before. No one around me seemed to understand what I was experiencing. The messages I received from family and friends were to stay quiet about my experience, to *move on* with my life, to *not think it*, and to *not talk* about it. I had to survive, and I knew I could not keep up the exhausting pace I held before. I wanted to be of service but was uncertain what that service looked like. I knew that public health was not really contributing to what I saw was the growing need to address the issue of suicide publicly. I decided to use my public health experience and my new knowledge as a "suicide survivor" to start working outside of public health, using the new interdisciplinary model that was being promoted by mental health experts to address the problem of suicide in the United States.

There were growing contingents of "suicide survivors" nationally who were mobilizing through grassroots organizations, such as the Suicide Prevention Action Network (SPAN USA), and inspiring me to do something in Ohio for suicide prevention. Using this public health–inspired cross-disciplinary approach, I founded the Ohio Coalition for Suicide Prevention and began doing a broad range of suicide prevention awareness events in the community and at Ohio State University, as well as advocating before the Ohio legislature and on television and radio. There was no real game plan but a feeling of urgency in my work. I was, like so many others who had been affected by suicide, fueled by a fire in my belly. SPAN's motto was "turning grief into action," and that is exactly what suicide survivors were doing nationally.

I moved to northern Virginia and began to work for the Kristen Brooks Hope Center, the administrative offices of 1-800-SUICIDE, the first national suicide prevention lifeline. For fourteen months, I worked as an administrator for this organization. My workdays were frequently twelve hours long, and I often worked seven days a week. I could not believe I was being paid to do work that I finally felt I was profoundly well suited for and prepared to do. It challenged me, and the personalities involved were large and difficult to manage.

Through a series of strange and certainly divinely instigated events, I found myself in a psychology master's degree program and then a clinical psychology PhD program, at Catholic University of America. I had an undergraduate degree in medieval and Renaissance studies, and I needed to return to school to transition to my new path, a new role that God was clearly fashioning for me. My research and faculty mentor, Dr. David Jobes, was and still is a profound influence, as were the loving, special people in his lab and in the Department of Psychology at Catholic University. I was in an incubator of learning and continued profound personal growth.

My personal life was transforming too. God brought people into my life who helped me personally and taught me that I could love and be loved again. The strength I felt was powerful. Still, the vulnerability created by traumatizing losses and pain from my husband's abandonment was also still very present. I was better able to balance those dichotomies and harness them. I was single-minded in my thoughts about the opportunities opening up and the need for people, like me, who wanted to serve clinically, and do research and advocacy work, but who also understood suicide from the inside out, as a suicide loss survivor.

POSTTRAUMATIC GROWTH

Through my studies, I was introduced to the new science on posttraumatic growth that described positive psychological changes in the aftermath of a shattering loss or trauma. Posttraumatic growth can manifest itself in several ways, including an increased appreciation for life, better interpersonal relationships, changed priorities, an increased sense of personal strength, and spiritual growth. Research has found that suicide-bereaved parents demonstrated moderate levels of posttraumatic growth despite their profound experiences of grief and loss. Posttraumatic growth has also been found in studies of military veterans and family members of active duty service members who died by suicide.

I finally had a name to put to my experience: posttraumatic growth. Mine was growth not in the absence of grief and loss but within the context of it. I was still processing my traumatizing experiences and growing intellectually, spiritually, and emotionally in ways that I was only beginning to appreciate. I thought back to those times when I would suffer with Christ on the Cross, kneeling at the altar in St. Patrick's Church in Columbus, Ohio, and offering my sorrow up in exchange for the promise of his body. I thought it was the only thing I had at the time. Little did I realize it was only just the beginning.

Key Points

- We need to find ways to talk about our grief with people who understand and are compassionate.
- Many people will not know what to say to us who are grieving a suicide. We need to be able to accept that reality.
- Turn to the saints and to spiritual practices to find meaning in your suffering and to transform your suffering into healing.
- There are many resources available to help you understand suicide and to learn how to be a suicide survivor.
- Suicide is traumatic, but you can experience "posttraumatic growth" and grow intellectually, spiritually, and emotionally.

Prayers for the Way

After praying one or more of these simple prayers, sit in silence and contemplate God's presence. Open your heart and mind to God's peace.

> God our Father,
> Like Job, I don't understand your ways
> especially why this suicide happened,
> but help me to accept your love and your healing.
> Amen.

Lord Jesus,
You suffered when people said things about you
that were harsh and untrue,
yet you forgave them and loved them.
Help me forgive and love those who do not know
how to talk to me
about my loved one's suicide. Amen.

Holy Spirit,
The Church has canonized many saints
who knew terrible circumstances and great pain.
Guide me to those who can help me understand
suffering and find peace and healing. Amen.

Mother Mary,
You survived the agonizing horror of watching your son
tortured and crucified.
Help me to survive the trauma of this suicide
and experience growth toward healing. Amen.

8.

The Journey from Suicide Loss to Assimilation

Tom and Fran Smith
Karla Smith Behavioral Health, Belleville, Illinois

Our twenty-six-year-old daughter, Karla, died by suicide on January 13, 2003. More precisely, her bipolar disorder took her life as cancer or heart disease takes many other lives. The experience of the Shoener family as described earlier in this book mirrors our story in most of the basic facts leading up to and immediately following Karla's death. Many of the emotions the Shoeners described we also felt, thirteen years earlier.

Our faith and parish community also soothed our stricken souls and played a major role in gently moving us from devastating loss to assimilating her death into the rest of our lives, which is how we describe our current status. For us, assimilation means we can fully participate in our daily lives: laughing at a joke, planning our next road trip, playing cards with friends, discussing politics, meditating in the morning, and even facilitating our support group meetings without an overwhelming sense of loss because of her death. We figure that's as good as it gets.

WE GRIEVE DIFFERENTLY—TOGETHER

Those early grief emotions—shock, loss, guilt, anger, frustration, rejection, depression, and loneliness—were unique in their intensity and attacked us simultaneously, like a pack of snarling wolves. We responded to this onslaught of feelings differently—Fran needing to talk about them and Tom wanting to isolate. She had a lot to say; he couldn't find his words. It took some months, but once we identified what was going on, we learned to respect each other's approach to this kind of grief. Eventually he found some words to express his reactions, initially through writing in a journal and then by writing a book about this family tragedy (*The Tattered Tapestry*). And she talked with others until Tom could untie the tangled emotional knots and join her. In time, the wolves slinked away, disappointed, and searched for more vulnerable prey.

KARLA'S FUNERAL STARTED OUR HEALING

The initial response to Karla's death from our diocese and parish was outstanding and comforting. Everyone knew how she died. Tom was the director of pastoral services for the Diocese of Belleville, Illinois, and Fran was principal of Queen of Peace Catholic Elementary School. Bishop Wilton Gregory (now Archbishop of Washington,

D.C.) cancelled a diocesan pastoral council meeting to participate in the funeral Mass and said some compassionate words.

Our pastor and friend Fr. Bill Hitpas was the celebrant and preached a remarkable homily on God joining us in our loss and pain. Kevin, Karla's twin brother and only sibling, spoke after Communion with a moving letter he wrote to his sister and invited the attendees, group by group, grievers from Oklahoma, Iowa, New Jersey, Wisconsin, and our local southern Illinois area, to rise in tribute to her life. The liturgical experience took us from our individual, private misery and gently engulfed us with care, understanding, and a tangible presence of God and the love of Jesus. That immediate tangible response has continued in multiple ways though the next sixteen years.

A CALL TO HELP OTHERS

Many people who came through the condolence line at Karla's wake mentioned that someone in their family or among their friends also struggled with a mental illness or died by suicide. Both of us, plus Kevin, were surprised at how frequently we heard these comments.

We decided then and there that we needed to do something about it. We pledged, with Karla in her coffin behind us, that we would create a way to assist people affected by mental illness or suicide and their families. Through the creative advice from a number of professionals, including our friend Fr. Charles Rubey and his Chicago-based L.O.S.S. program, we gradually refined our mission to supporting families affected by mental illness and suicide. Two years later we formed a nonprofit organization now called Karla

Smith Behavioral Health (KSBH; www.karlasmithbehavioralhealth.
org) to fulfill that pledge.

What we learned through KSBH and its many services is that a
ministry like this provides concrete help for thousands of people, but
it is also an emotional and spiritual resource for us. Through prayer,
spiritual direction, and meditation we have come to see that serving
others with these issues is our personal and specific way to live out
the Gospel message to love our neighbors, especially those in need.
Fran provides a mentoring service to many people struggling with
issues related to mental illness and suicide loss, while Tom is active as
a member of the board of directors and does multiple public presen-
tations on these themes. While our organization is not a designated,
Catholic-related ministry, we are comfortable in thinking about it
in those terms. The secular and the sacred intermingle, especially in
terms of service to others.

OUR PARISH SUPPORTS OUR FAITH AND GRIEF

Over the years our parish community has consistently enriched our
growth in faith, nourishing our grief work through multiple individual and group experiences. Fr. Bill became a compassionate and
effective spiritual director and counselor, offering insight into the
grief that clouded our judgment about everything and assuring us
that even our negative feelings such as guilt and anger were normal.

We have been part of a small faith group sponsored by the
parish for about twenty years, predating Karla's death. Over these
years we have become close friends and shared our life experiences,
including the death of family members, personal health issues such

as cancer and multiple operations, an automobile accident, marriages of children, and births of grandchildren. We meet about twice a month to search for and find how God is present within our lives, comforting us in the sad times and celebrating with us in the good times. Through those friendships, we have met the ongoing presence of Jesus. The wisdom in the group reflects the wisdom of Jesus. We have studied our faith, clarifying what we believe and inspiring one another by sharing our life experiences through spiritual books and videos, and asking the questions that shape our spiritual journeys. We are not alone.

Many of the people in this small faith group also join a larger gathering each Sunday morning between Masses for our Dialogue with the Word program. Once again, the faith convictions of these people help break open the scripture readings of the day, and we are nourished and guided not only by the scripture texts themselves but also by the way these devoted Catholics apply that message to their lives. It is another opportunity for us to deepen our trust in the loving presence of our God who continues to comfort us in our ongoing sense of loss due to Karla's suicide.

There is no getting over her death, but we can get *through* that grief, even though the most intense part of that loss is thankfully behind us. We still miss her, of course, because a young death implies that we grieve the future that will never be—milestones that will never be experienced, such as a wedding, grandchildren, her husband, her career, or whatever she would have done or become. Flashes of what might have been still haunt us. Our participation in the small faith group and the Dialogue with the Word program offer a consistent community of faith-inspired friends who help cushion the grief and create an accepting atmosphere and a culture of understanding, comfort, and support.

Once a year on the Sunday closest to her date of death, one of the weekend Masses is for Karla. It is a memorial for us and, in a specific way, helps us focus on the death and resurrection of Jesus as a prelude to Karla's resurrected life, where the effects of her bipolar no longer interfere with her generous and loving spirit. At this Mass and throughout the year, there are often prayers of intercession with mental health and suicide themes. And Fr. Bill often includes mental illness in his always-inspiring and enlightening homilies. We take great comfort in these public liturgical expressions of the compassion of Jesus and the sacramental presence of Christ.

The parish also promotes a unique "To Be Given Away" program, which is one of the many opportunities to donate to worthy causes as part of our parish tithing efforts. Everyone is invited to put some of their donation dollars into this program. The result is that parishioners vote on how the money gathered gets distributed to local causes. Our Karla Smith Behavioral Health organization has received funds each year from this generous and creative program. The support from the Church is not only spiritual and emotional but also financial and helps us offer our services to more people. In fact, we use that money as scholarships for parishioners who need our help. Our gratitude for this financial contribution is profound and deepens our personal ties to this faith community.

ACCEPTING POWERLESSNESS AND ASSIMILATING KARLA'S DEATH INTO OUR LIVES

What we have learned is that the death of Karla has pushed us into the world of powerlessness. We are haunted occasionally by what we might have done to intervene in her suicide and, in our worst times, felt guilt and regret for not being there to stop her—possibly. We now know and accept that, all things considered, we did what we could do at the time.

We professed our love for her and told her we would support her and be with her in her deep depression, but in the end, we could not penetrate the darkness of her desperate sense of aloneness. We could not assure her enough that she was not a burden to us that we could not handle. In the end, she felt alone, a burden, and could see no other way to release the emotional, psychological, and spiritual pain that ate away at her resolve to live. Her suicide was, to her, the only way to relieve her suffering. And at that final moment, we were powerless to change her confused and misguided mind.

We wish we would have learned the depths of this powerlessness some other way. But we now know we are powerless in other areas of life as well, and this perspective has matured us and guides us in these other areas. We judge others less. We empathize more quickly and at a greater depth. We identify immediately with other suicide survivors. Our lives have better priorities. We have discovered more depth in our love for each other. Our faith has taken on another dimension. Our work with KSBH is fueled by our desire to lessen the pain suffered by others who are faced with mental illness or suicide.

OUR CATHOLIC FAITH IS EMBODIED IN OUR PARISH AND COMMUNITY

In the final analysis, we want our daughter back. We are still assimilating. But the last twenty years have taught us some things that we might not have learned. We are grateful for the learning but sad that we learned it in the mental illness and suicide classroom. And we are also thankful that this classroom was in the Catholic school of life.

All of this exposure to our Catholic faith provides us with a constant presence of the core messages of Christianity: the daily awareness of the reign of God as proclaimed by Jesus, the ongoing reality of transforming death into resurrection as initiated by Jesus, the anticipation of a blessed eternal life, the compassion of a loving God, the redemptive potential of suffering, and the saving power of Jesus' life and teaching.

These core Catholic teachings are more than consoling and comforting doctrines. They are embodied in our friends, leaders, and faith companions in our parish programs and help guide us to peace, consolation, and the courage to face another tomorrow with confidence and hope. Over the years, this lived message becomes the ocean we swim in and the purified water we drink.

Key Points

- Karla Smith was a beautiful young woman who died by suicide brought on by bipolar disorder.
- We have learned to understand and respect each other's different ways of grieving and have accepted our powerlessness as we assimilate Karla's death into our lives.
- Karla's funeral liturgy took us from our individual, private misery and gently engulfed us with care, understanding, and a tangible presence of God.
- Our parish regularly incorporates into liturgies prayers for those living with mental illness and who have died by suicide.

- Our parish has provided support to us in our grief and in our efforts to help others with programs and tangible support in ways that embody our Catholic faith.

Prayers for the Way

After praying one or more of these simple prayers, sit in silence and contemplate God's presence. Open your heart and mind to God's peace.

God our Father,
Lead me into the depths of the liturgy
to feel your healing presence at Mass. Amen.

Lord Jesus Christ,
You humbled yourself
and "became obedient unto death."
Give me the humility to accept my powerlessness
so that I learn to live with my loved one's suicide. Amen.

Holy Spirit,
Instruct and guide the Church, especially my parish,
to find ways to pray for and support
those who live with a mental illness
and for those who grieve a suicide. Amen.

Mother Mary,
You understand the dynamics of family life;
give me the grace to understand that we all
grieve differently
so that I can comfort my spouse, my children, my
siblings, and all members of my family as they grieve.
And help me to understand and accept my own way of
grieving. Amen.

Closing Reflection

Bishop John Dolan
Diocese of San Diego

Suicide affects us all. The lives of survivors of victims of suicide—parents, children, siblings, friends, coworkers, and parishioners—are forever altered. The chapters in this small book have touched on the Church's response to the morality of suicide and the stigma and shame that many of you face when grieving the suicide of your loved one. These reflections go beyond the mere theological and moral constructs regarding suicide and touch on the raw human emotions surrounding this troubling reality that we are facing on an ever-increasing basis.

Pope Francis's call to *accompaniment* can never be more on point when dealing with the harsh reality of mental disorders, depression, and suicide. As a Church, we must embrace this challenge to accompany our brothers and sisters who struggle just as we do. Accompanying is not easy. It requires patience and a lot of love. Not only does the Church accompany and offer prayerful support for those of us who grieve the loss of a loved one to suicide, but also the Church accompanies those who have died by suicide with prayers for their eternal repose.

The Church stands guard with those who grieve the suicide of a loved one, and we keep vigil for those who have died by suicide. After all, long before we stood watch over our loved ones, God had a watchful eye over them. Though some struggled to believe in God who could save them, God never stopped believing in them. Maybe they had no hope in the Lord, but God always had great hope for them. And maybe they could not love themselves sufficiently, but Jesus supplied more than enough love for them as they struggled on their journey.

We all have heard the song from the Beatles "Do You Want to Know a Secret?" It includes the words, "Let me whisper in your ear . . . I'm in love with you." That is certainly a secret worth bragging about. And as a Church, we have been proclaiming this secret for more than two thousand years. It needs to be proclaimed from the housetops or whispered into the ears of those we love regularly. Let God say, "I'm in love with you!"

Unfortunately, as often and loudly as this has been broadcast, many of us still do not hear this voice of love. Often, those who died by suicide struggled to know the depth of God's love for them. They struggled to love themselves.

We know the reasons that may lead a person to suicide. Mental disorder is chief among the reasons for a majority of suicides. Crippling addictions and even situational issues involving breakups or financial distress also lead some to take their lives. Due to these illnesses and circumstances, they could not hear the many voices (including God's) who said, "I'm in love with you."

As part of the Church, we continue to share this Gospel of love with our loved ones who have died through suicide. The Mass is offered as a prayer of love for those whose lives ended so tragically. We know they struggled and were afflicted, but they, like us, are all children of a God of love. There is no judgment here. As St. James says, we "show no partiality" (Jas 2:1). We only show love: love for our loved one who is deceased, love for other brothers and sisters who died by suicide, love for their family and friends, and love for all.

Jesus once said, "Remain in my love" (Jn 15:9) so we might have joy and so our joy would be complete. Who wants incomplete joy? Complete joy comes from putting Christ first always. Abiding in his love brings us joyful fulfillment, which begets greater love from family and friends.

Abiding in the love of Christ in Word and sacrament at Mass is a perfect way to prayerfully support our loved ones who have died by suicide. The Eucharist is the source and summit of the love that we share with each other and with those who have died by suicide. Responding to Christ's call to follow him and to abide in him allows us to find consolation and provide perfect and lasting love and support. Christ offers us the peace to endure the pain and to prayerfully consider the mystery of suicide, especially as we contemplate the death and resurrection of the Lord himself.

Putting the Lord first, we trust that our loved ones are greeted in the loving arms of Jesus. They now abide with him. He grants to them complete joy—without pain of mental disorder, addictions, or other situational realities that led them to suicide.

Let us continue to accompany our loved ones who died by suicide and entrust their souls to the Lord. May they rest in peace.

Key Points

- You are not alone in grieving a suicide. Suicide affects us all.
- Pope Francis's call to *accompaniment* can never be more on point when dealing with the harsh reality of mental disorders, depression, and suicide.
- Though some who died by suicide may have struggled to believe in God who could save them, God never stopped believing in them.

- As a Church, we share this Gospel of love with our loved ones who have died through suicide. We know they struggled and were afflicted, but they, like us, are all children of a God of love.
- Abiding in the love of Christ in Word and sacrament at Mass is a perfect way to prayerfully support those who have died by suicide.

Prayers for the Way

After praying one or more of these simple prayers, sit in silence and contemplate God's presence. Open your heart and mind to God's peace.

> God our Father,
> Although my loved one may have struggled to believe
> in a God who could save him [her],
> you never stopped believing in him [her].
> Even in my sadness, help me to share the Gospel of love
> wherever and whenever I have the chance. Amen.
>
> Lord Jesus,
> You invited us to abide in your love.
> Teach me to pray for and with [name]
> and to have complete faith in the promise
> of your Resurrection. Amen.
>
> Holy Spirit,
> Guide your Church and all its members to patiently
> accompany those who struggle with suicidal thoughts.
> Comfort us who grieve the suicide of a loved one.
> Help us keep in our prayers all who have died
> by suicide. Amen.

Mother Mary,
Carry my loved one who died by suicide
into the loving arms of your son Jesus.
Ask your son to grant her [him] complete joy,
without the pain of heart and mind that led to suicide.
Amen.

Resources

Books

Alar, Chris, and Jason Lewis, *After Suicide: There's Hope for Them and for You*. Stockbridge, MA: Marian Press, 2019.

Bishops of California. *Hope and Healing: A Pastoral Letter from the Bishops of California on Caring for those Who Suffer from Mental Illness*. Sacramento, CA: California Catholic Conference, 2018.

Clemons, James T. *What Does the Bible Say about Suicide?* Minneapolis, MN: Fortress Press, 1990.

D'Arcy, Paula. *Winter of the Heart, Finding Your Way through the Mystery of Grief*. Notre Dame, IN: Ave Maria Press, 2018.

Guntzelman, Joan. *God Knows You're Grieving*. Notre Dame, IN: Ave Maria Press, 2001.

Koenig-Bricker, Woodeene. *Meditations for Those Left Behind by Suicide*. New London, CT: Twenty-Third Publications, 2018.

Rolheiser, Ron. *Bruised and Wounded: Struggling to Understand Suicide*. Brewster, MA: Paraclete Press, 2017.

Ross, E. Betsy. *After Suicide: A Ray of Hope for Those Left Behind*. Cambridge, MA: Perseus, 1997.

Rupp, Joyce. *Praying Our Goodbyes: A Spiritual Companion Through Life's Losses and Sorrows.* Notre Dame, IN: Ave Maria Press, 2013.

Woelfel, Joni. *Meditations for Survivors of Suicide*. Totowa, NJ, Resurrection Press, 2002.

Wolfelt, Alan D. *Finding the Words: How to Talk with Children and Teens About Death, Suicide, Homicide.* Fort Collins, CO: Companion Press, 2013.

Wolfelt, Alan D. *The Wilderness of Suicide Grief: Finding Your Way (Understanding Your Grief).* Fort Collins, CO: Companion Press, 2010.

Websites

Alliance of Hope for Suicide Loss Survivors. https://allianceofhope.org.

American Foundation for Suicide Prevention. I've Lost Someone. https://afsp.org/ive-lost-someone.

Association of Catholic Mental Health Ministers. http://www.catholicmhm.org.

The Dougy Center, The National Center for Grieving Children and Families. https://www.dougy.org.

Loving Outreach to Survivors of Suicide. Based in Chicago. LOSS offers hope and healing to those who mourn a loss to suicide. https://www.catholiccharities.net/GetHelp/OurServices/Counseling/Loss.aspx#:~:text=Loving%20Outreach%20to%20Survivors%20of,talk%20about%20feelings%20and%20experiences.

National Action Alliance for Suicide Prevention: Faith.Hope.Life. A campaign aimed at involving every faith community in suicide prevention. https://theactionalliance.org/faith-hope-life.

National Catholic Partnership on Disability. Council on Mental Illness: Suicide. https://ncpd.org/disabilities-ministries-specific-disabilities-mental-illness/suicide.

Nouwen Network: About Suicide. http://nouwen-network.com/aboutsuicide.html.

Suicide Prevention Resource Center: Provide for Immediate and
    Long-Term Postvention. http://www.sprc.org/comprehensive-
    approach/postvention.
Survivors of Suicide Loss (SOSL): Resources. Based in San Diego.
    SOSL reaches out to and supports people who have lost a loved
    one to suicide. https://www.soslsd.org/resources.
Tragedy Assistance Program for Survivors (TAPS) provides comfort,
    care and resources to all those grieving the death of a military
    loved one. https://www.taps.org/suicide.
Waterloo Catholics – Resources for Suicide Survivors. https://water-
    loocatholics.org/resources-for-suicide-survivors.

Notes

1. Colby Itkowitz, "She 'Loved Life': A Grieving Father Wrote Openly about Suicide and Mental Illness in Daughter's Obituary," *Washington Post*, August 17, 2016, https://www.washingtonpost.com.

2. Rui Antunes, "Katie Committed Suicide in a Bipolar Crisis and Her Father Wrote in the Obituary a Message to Humanity," *Visão*, August 26, 2016, https://visao.sapo.pt.

3. Simone Olivero, "Parents Use Daughter's Obituary to Discuss the Stigmas around Mental Health," *Yahoo News*, August 9, 2016, https://www.yahoo.com.

4. Sharon Grigsby, "Grieving Father's Commonsense Message about Mental Illness Is a Wake-Up Call," *Dallas Morning News*, August 18, 2016, https://www.dallasnews.com.

5. Andrea Monaci, "She Loved Life—a Father in Mourning Writes of the Suicide of Daughter with a Mental Illness," *Urban Post*, August 20, 2016, https://urbanpost.it.

6. Greg Kandra, "On the Deacon's Daughter Who Committed Suicide: 'God Will Use This Death to Help Others Come Out of the Shadows,'" *Deacons Bench* (blog), Aleteia, August 17, 2016, https://aleteia.org/blogs/deacon-greg-kandra/on-the-deacons-daughter-who-committed-suicide-god-will-use-this-death-to-help-others-come-out-of-the-shadows.

7. Aimee Meade, "This Father Used His Daughter's Obituary to Make an Important Point about the Way We Treat People with

Mental Health Issues," *Independent,* August 23, 2016, Indy100, https://www.indy100.com.

8. "Kathleen Marie Shoener, died 3 August 2016," Legacy.com, https://www.legacy.com/obituaries/name/kathleen-shoener-obituary?pid=180989005.

9. For more development on this, see Ronald Rolheiser, "For Understanding How We Remain in Contact with Our Loved Ones after Their Deaths," in *The Holy Longing: The Search for Christian Spirituality* (New York: Random House, 2014), 104–6.

10. Substance Abuse and Mental Health Services Administration (SAMHSA), Center for Behavioral Health Statistics and Quality, *Key Substance Use and Mental Health Indicators in the United States: Results from the 2017 National Survey on Drug Use and Health,* HHS Pub. No. SMA 17-5068, NSDUH Series H-53 (Rockville, MD: Author, 2018).

11. Ibid.

12. Edwin S. Shneidman, *Definition of Suicide* (New York: Wiley, 1985), 202–13.

The Association of Catholic Mental Health Ministers is a lay association whose members walk with people living with a mental illness and their families to help them find the support and services that they need. ACMHM members work to eliminate the stigma and discrimination that people living with a mental illness encounter in the Church and in the world. Members strive to strengthen mental health ministry in the Catholic Church by networking and sharing resources.

www.catholicmhm.org

Ed Shoener was ordained a permanent deacon in 2004 and serves at St. Peter's Cathedral in the Diocese of Scranton. He is a founding member of the Association of Catholic Mental Health Ministers, the Catholic Institute of Mental Health Ministry at the University of San Diego, and the Scranton Mental Health Ministry. He serves on the boards of the Council on Mental Illness, National Catholic Partnership on Disability, and Pathways to Promise. He earned a graduate certificate in spiritual direction from the Aquinas Institute of Theology.

Shoener is president of Shoener Environmental Consulting. He has a bachelor of science degree in environmental research management from Penn State University, where he also earned a master's degree in environmental protection control.

Shoener's family and friends founded The Katie Foundation after his daughter, Kathleen, died by suicide in 2016. The obituary he wrote for her went viral. The Shoeners live in Scranton, Pennsylvania.

catholicmhm.org
thekatiefoundation.org
Facebook: The Katie Foundation

Most Rev. John P. Dolan is auxiliary bishop of San Diego. He also serves the diocese as vicar general, moderator of the curia, and vicar for clergy. Ordained to the priesthood in 1989, Dolan became auxiliary bishop in 2017.

He is the chaplain of the Lost Boys of Sudan, a member of the Catholic Institute for Mental Health Ministry, and a board member of Father Joe's Villages, a ministry to the homeless. Dolan earned his bachelor's degree in philosophy from the University of San Diego and master's degrees in divinity and theology from St. Patrick's Seminary in Menlo Park, California. He is the author of *Rose of Lima: A Nine-Day Study of Her Life* and *Who is Like God? A Nine-Day Journey with St. Michael.*

www.sdcatholic.org/bishops/auxiliary-bishop-dolan

A Pastoral Handbook for Catholic Leaders

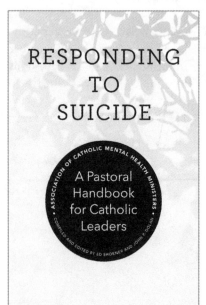

Many pastoral leaders feel ill-equipped to respond to the turmoil of those who face the death by suicide of a loved one. *Responding to Suicide* is the first book written for Catholic leaders that takes a holistic approach to understanding suicide and ministering effectively in its aftermath.

More than a dozen leading mental health practitioners, Catholic theologians, and pastoral care experts share how best to respond to suicide as leaders in parishes, schools, healthcare systems, and other Church settings. The book offers a cross-disciplinary approach that provides basic information about the central role of mental health in suicide and clarifies Church teaching about suicide, funerals and burials for those who have died by suicide, and their afterlife.

"So much misunderstanding surrounds Catholics and suicide, which is precisely why this book is not just very good, it is essential for those of us charged with the pastoral care of God's people."

—Fr. Joshua J. Whitfield

Pastoral Administrator
St. Rita Catholic Community and School
Dallas, Texas